THE
DARK SIDE
OF
LEADERSHIP

—

A Cautionary Fable for Those
Who Serve as Trustees or Directors
On Not-For-Profit Boards

CHARLES G. BEAUDETTE

Copyright © 2012 Charles G. Beaudette
All rights reserved.

ISBN: 1439280258
ISBN-13: 9781439280256

Library of Congress Cataloging-in-Publication Data
is available upon request.

Published in the United States by
C.G. Beaudette, South Bristol, Maine 04568, USA.

PRINTED IN THE UNITED STATES OF AMERICA

10 9 8 7 6 5 4 3

First Edition

Beaudette offers advice complementary to that of motivational speakers and writers. Advice is aimed at those Board members faced with difficult, unresponsive, or desultory behavior. In an engaging narrative form, he demonstrates the subtle (and not so suitable) initial moves that signal a covert takeover of management. This book should be of real value and assistance to new as well as seasoned Board members.

> —Robert F. Preti, Esq. (now retired) practiced law for some 50 years and was a founding partner of Preti Flaherty Beliveau and Pachios, LLP, of Portland and Augusta (Maine), Concord (NH), and Boston.

Beaudette's book offers Trustees and Directors the warning flags of a covert Board takeover. His tale offers vivid and specific examples that a manipulator might use to disrupt collegial governance. This book's recommendations of available responses fill a vacuum in the leadership bookshelf.

> —David C. Smith, recently retired executive officer of the Council of Presidents, New England Land-Grant Universities (Universities of Connecticut, of Maine, Massachusetts Amherst, New Hampshire, Rhode Island, and Vermont).

Using experience as a springboard, Charles Beaudette has provided a timely message about leadership in an unusually arresting format. This book should be required reading for all inexperienced and many experienced individuals asked to assume the responsibilities of leadership on any Board. Whether you are flattered by appointment to such a position, or frustrated by similar efforts in the past, resolve your confusion. Read this book.

> — J. Howard Hannemann, A.B., M.D., FACR

This book is dedicated to those who have fought the good battle to maintain decency in the conduct of the public's affairs.

DISCLAIMER

The material in this book is for informational purposes only. As each individual situation is unique, the reader should use proper discretion, possibly in consultation with an attorney, before undertaking actions or using techniques described in this book. The author and publisher expressly disclaim responsibility for any adverse results that may result from the use or application of the information contained in this book.

The cautionary-fable story told herein is a pedagogic work of fiction drawn in part from a lifetime of reading about, and experience with, committees and boards of various types. Each dialog is fabricated for its immediate purpose, each actor is necessarily a blending of characters, each action results from a blending of purposes, and the story itself is an invention. Latent resemblances to actual persons, places, or events are coincidental and unavoidable.

Table of Contents

Opening Note   1

Characters   5

1.	The First Two Steps	7
	Note 1: End of Collegiality	15
2.	Getting Acquainted	17
	Note 2: Intimidation	23
3.	The Replacement	25
	Note 3: A Confederacy	33
4.	A Setup	35
	Note 4: Picking the Fruit	43
5.	First Awareness	45
	Note 5: Spotting Takeovers	55
6.	The Confederacy	57
	Note 6: Rhetorical Leadership	63
7.	The Slate	65
	Note 7: The Extended Presidency	71
8.	Elections	73
	Note 8: A Disabled GC	79

9.	That Woman	81
	Note 9: Subordination	89
10.	Harness Fitting	91
	Note 10: Harness Fitting	95
11.	A Third Resignee	97
	Note 11: Shortened Terms	105
12.	Cleaning Up	107
	Note 12: Heightened Awareness	113
13.	Coming of Age	115
	Note 13: A Public Assault	123
14.	A Member Governs	125
	Note 14: The Uses of Untruth	131
15.	Another Removal	133
	Note 15: The Eavesdropper	141
16.	Moving On	143
	Note 16: Weakness Advanced	153
17.	Piling On	155
	Note 17: Spontaneous Response	163
18.	Harassment	165
	Note 18: Working Outside the Box	173
19.	One More to Go	175
Closing Note		181
Acknowledgments		187
Author Biography		188

Opening Note

"It can't be done!" That's what they say.

Yet, it is done. A member of a Board of Trustees takes over a Board's governance role for himself while other members remain unaware. "The Dark Side of Leadership" reveals, by means of a fictional story, how a trustee member covertly manipulates a Board of twenty members. That story includes the cunning removal of targeted members by subtle means, some clandestine, possibly unethical, and even cruel.

Such conduct continues over a period of years extending beyond the term of office of the Board's officers, and does so without the trustees gaining recognition of this illicit activity. "Notes" which accompany this story explain how Board members can recognize warning flags and how they might thwart such actions.

Through dialog, this story reveals the methods used, event by event, over a period of two years. How the story's protagonist, initially the Board's president, deals to himself the necessary cards and then plays them deftly, if somewhat brutally, to achieve control of institution policy. Other trustees remain annoyed, puzzled, ignorant, and helpless. Such an activity may be casually referred to as a "takeover."

A town council, a community college, fraternity, museum, orchestra, Masonic group, opera company, Knights of Columbus chapter, or parish church all face this possibility. Nonprofit, not-for-profit, or local governmental institutions — small enough that they do not interest those who serve on Boards professionally — attract members who are parents, artists, local professionals, local industrial managers, community leaders, and so forth.

Bookstores that serve upscale urban and suburban communities fill many bookcases with leadership books. These are optimistic books concerned with what might be described as "How to be a good leader," and "How to repair or avoid other member's lack of leadership skills." No books, apparently, describe how a Board of Trustees may be undone quite deliberately by one of its members. Such a trustee would be especially competent in leadership skills. He also would harbor a concealed agenda for the advancement of which he covertly redirects the organization's members and activities. However that may be, this book does not set pessimism as an alternative attitude. It offers merely a cautionary tale describing what others have run into on occasion, along with suggestions to prepare an aspiring leader to recognize and respond to a particular class of difficulties.

Our story tells how this trustee, our protagonist, not only removes from the Board those members capable of compromising his purpose, but also selects less than competent members to fill important positions, thereby establishing an hegemony of his influence over it. Once established, the protagonist maintains this control even for several years beyond his own term of office. This is accomplished with a sequence of careful moves such that no alarm is raised against him. By following the action as it is presented in the form of dialog, word by word, the reader learns what to look for, how to recognize significant symptoms, and what actions might be taken in self-defense.

This book does not teach how to accomplish a takeover. As recognized in these pages, the takeover of a Board requires exceptional leadership virtuosity, a capability, for example, to accurately evaluate individuals on short notice, to fill important offices with presentable but unqualified candidates used as placeholders, and to quickly change an associate's opinion on some small matter. The question of how to fulfill such skill requirements is a topic that resides beyond the reach of this book.

Leadership books usually run the instructional text from page to page and from cover to cover, placing the examples of wrong behavior separately, often in text boxes. For our topic, however, a different or inside-out, arrangement seems better. Where covert leadership necessarily is highly integrated within the social milieu of the Board, the most efficient presentation of bad behavior takes the form of one continuous story that extends through the nineteen chapters. The explanatory, or instructional, part of the book occupies separate notes which appear after each chapter and as opening and closing commentary.

This book addresses itself to the victims and their peers who suffer as trustees while strange maneuvers float about them. They find themselves helpless to understand those maneuvers and to respond effectively. The notes teach what to watch for, what response might be helpful, and what to guard against in the way of retribution should members try inhibiting the protagonist's purpose.

Our example, for this story, is a Board of Trustees of a secondary school, a private Academy ensconced in a still- expanding suburb of a city in the

Opening Note

northwest part of the United States. In the late nineteenth century the location was an extensive cattle ranch, and the city was a railroad-stop town some fifteen miles away. The town grew into a city, and the city grew suburbs that eventually reached and surrounded the ranch. Ranching became less commercially advantageous, and the ranching operation sold its land piece by piece for suburban development. But while ranching suffered, it seemed that the suburbs loved horses — for casual riding and for competitive exhibition. In response, the ranch started a horseback riding school that evolved into an equestrian academy offering world-class competitive instruction.

In the mid-nineteen hundreds, classroom buildings were added for the use of full-time riding students. Those quickly evolved into a sixth grade through high school curriculum, and within another decade boasted college preparatory accreditation. The combined academic and riding schools, with their land and buildings, were eventually converted into a modestly endowed not-for-profit operation: an Academy and riding school, governed by a Board of Trustees.

As our story begins, the Academy is steeped in and, to a large extent, bound by a century of steady success. The academic and riding activities perform near the top of their fields. The governing Board has twenty trustee members, each upon election to serve a three year term. Most are parents of students, and have been selected slightly for wealth and professional skills. Also on the Board, as school outreach to the community, is the local state representative, and as a courtesy, an attorney who is a personal friend of the school's headmaster, a position for whom the bylaws do not provide a place on the Board. It is well understood, however, that nothing happens at the school without the headmaster's involvement and commitment.

Operation of the Board is casual. The nine pages of bylaws are now of uncertain date. They call for the Board to follow Robert's Rules of Order, an instruction that is mostly honored in the breach. Its schedule follows the academic calendar, meeting during the first week of the month from October through June, except for January. At the June meeting, its two officers, the president and the chair of the governance committee, are elected for the next academic year. The president is given the usual powers of appointment, agenda setting, and ex-officio membership on all committees. The office of GC chair is an elected office to give it a parallel authority with that of the president.

While it is the president's job to lead the effort to govern the Academy by setting policy, it is the chair of the governance committee's job to watch that, in doing so, the president works within the bylaws and customs of the Academy. If the chair finds something out of line, he takes it to his committee for review, confirmation, and a vote to undertake corrective action. Additionally, the GC, besides exercising its general role for personnel oversight, has responsibility to evaluate and nominate new trustees, and to prepare a slate of the two officer nominations for the annual meeting in June.

At the opening of our story, it is annual meeting time. The Academy has its affairs well in order. The Board's GC is composed of four long-time members, the most recent past president, and the two current officers. For the meeting, they have prepared a well-considered slate of two energetic, intelligent, and competent members for election as Board officers for the coming academic year.

Characters

The characters that make up our story are listed here by chapter:

01) Robert Talent, newly elected president, the protagonist;
Jack Medford, newly elected chair of the GC;
Greta Johnson, new Board member, newly appointed to GC;
Cator Blackworthy, member, and state representative;

02) Anthony Petrillo, staff, Academy headmaster;
Daniel Goodacre, staff, Academy accounts manager;
Frederick Jacobs, member, friend of the headmaster;
Creston Langmuir, candidate, member, problem for Talent;
Pierre de Vanough, chair budget c., old friend of Talent;
Wilson, history teacher, chair of the faculty;

03) Talbot Train, Board consultant, old friend of Talent;
John Stoddart, replacement chair of the GC;
Elaine Rutherford Blandley, new member, old friend Talent;
Ruth Blanchard, member, old friend of Talent;
Roger Papalian, member, immediate past president of the Board;

04) Mrs. Snow, senior staff, admissions director;
Beth Perwick, member, sole candidate for next president;

05) Theresa Peterson, distinguished and generous member;

06) Jacob "Jake" Isaac, member, accountant;

09) Rexford Lake, member;

10) Dorothy Huang, faculty, chair of math dept.;

13) Richard Pomentare, local dentist, member;

16) Phil Penrose, member;

17) Barbara Antlower, parent, member;

1. The First Two Steps

PREEMPTION

The Academy's trustees, so far, have actively and successfully addressed themselves to school governance. The occasion is their annual meeting in June. The Board has just voted into office the nomination slate for its two officers, Robert Talent as president, and Jack Medford as chair of the governance committee, without contest from the floor.

Robert Talent is an urbane attorney of modest demeanor, professionally secure as a partner of a firm in the city center. He has been a member of the Board for three years serving quietly and commendably on the building and grounds committee, and in the past year as its chair. His son is a junior in the high school and a star at competitive riding. He does not speak at Board meetings unless in the way of brief statements regarding his duties, or to give his careful judgment on a point when asked for it. While he is not a gregarious person, his considerable diligence and competence are well recognized.

Jack Medford, a home construction contractor, takes seriously his responsibilities as a Board member. As chair of the program committee he engaged fully in discussions of Board matters and volunteered hours of his time when asked. He has two daughters in middle school, both smitten with the work of caring for and riding horses. As the new chair of the Board's most important committee, he appreciates his responsibility as overseer of the Board's functioning and how it manages itself.

As the meeting drew to a close, Medford waited about in anticipation of a brief introductory chat with the new president who was continuously engaged with other members and with one of whom he eventually disappeared through a door. Nor in subsequent days did Medford receive a telephone call or e-mail from the president, who avoids text messaging of every kind for most matters, preferring to engage each individual spontaneously in person or over the phone. Medford could not help but notice from indications within the school that Talent was thoroughly busy with his new responsibilities. Out of a sense of deference, Medford presumed that he would be contacted by the president when the time was ripe.

But the time to ripen became the whole summer. Medford was disappointed that he did not have an opportunity to plan with the president the appointment of his committee members before September arrived. He had as yet heard nothing and there were only three weeks remaining until the Board's first meeting in October.

He placed a call to Robert Talent's office, not wanting to bother him at home, but he was not in. He left a voice message explaining that he was ready to discuss a list of prospective names for his committee. He was troubled to get no return call during the following week.

With two weeks remaining, he called Talent at home. "Good evening, Bob," he said hesitantly, "this is Jack Medford. I've been trying to reach you."

"Are you not planning to be at our October Board meeting on Tuesday, the fourth?" Talent asked.

"Oh, yes, of course, I . . ." said Medford.

"Well, we can talk there, can't we?"

"Yes, but I thought . . ."

"I'll see you there, Jack, and we'll have a chance to talk. Good night, now." In this abrupt manner, the president brought the call to a swift end.

Medford was hurt. He thought, "Bob will be busy at the meeting; there will be no time for us to select members for the committee — I think five would be the right number. There's a tradition at the Academy to include the immediate past president — Roger Papalian. Some long-term members are needed — they know where the bodies are buried — but they may be committed to other committees by this late date. Damn it all!

"What on Earth is going on? I can't believe he hasn't had time to talk with me since last June. Not word number one. Maybe, if I have my list of names ready, he'll just rubber-stamp it. He would have time for that at the meeting. I'll have to try for that."

Jack Medford arrived early for the first Board meeting. It was held in an open lounge area of the school on a Tuesday evening at seven. There were no other activities in the building so they had the place to themselves. About twenty members would be present plus the headmaster, and maybe a senior administrative staff member, both as guests. Medford knew them well, and received due recognition for his new role as an officer of the Board.

1. The First Two Steps

At seven sharp, the president walked in, marched to the head of the circle of tables, invited the recording secretary to sit beside him, and called the Board to order.

An agenda had been e-mailed to members previously by the secretary showing mostly organizational matters and announcements, nothing of substance. The president, in a soft, genial voice, thanked everyone for coming, remarked how he looked forward to the new year, and the many matters waiting to be taken up.

He then invited the headmaster to speak, who offered five minutes of graceful generalities about the school operation, how it was well underway, mutual interests of the school and the Board, and how he, too, looked forward to an exciting year ahead.

First business concerned the organization of the Board, how it would be structured with its many committees, the chairmanship and membership of each. The president asked the secretary to go around the circle to pass out a sheet of paper to each depicting the new committee structure.

Medford became agitated. He wondered what was coming at him. "How could that paper be prepared when the most important committee has not yet been planned?" he thought. "Could Bob have put his own selection of members on it without discussion with me? That would be a slap in the face." He got his copy at last, and his committee appeared right there at the top of the chart. It showed himself as the chair and with just two members. The first was the president, ex-officio; the other was Greta Johnson, a name he did not recognize.

"Who is she," he wondered, "and how did she get on my committee without my knowing of her?" He raised his head and looked around at the circle of members. No one else was looking around. He thought of walking over to the president to ask the meaning of his committee listing. No, with the Board expecting continuance, he couldn't do that. "I'll have to wait and see," he realized, "but how humiliating it is to learn about my committee along with everyone else. It's a deliberate insult for Bob not to have informed me beforehand. It means our phone conversation the other evening was flim-flam."

Talent brought the meeting along efficiently and yet considerately. It moved promptly from item to item of its agenda. None of it pertained to the governance committee. At one point, the president asked if there was anything more for the meeting to consider.

Cator Blackworthy's hand went up.

"We have not heard any committee reports."

"We don't have time for them tonight," the president responded, and nothing more was said on the subject.

The president eventually spoke of events planned for the fall, reminded them of the date for their November meeting, and adjourned the assembly.

Listening to the president, Medford was struck by his lack of presence in speaking to the assembly. He perceived that the president had difficulty speaking to a group, and that he was careful to say as little as possible.

CONFUSION

As the meeting broke up, Medford was beside himself with humiliation. If members were to speak to him about his tiny committee, what could he say? "I had no part in it." How embarrassing. Fortunately, no one else seemed interested in his committee. Without incidental conversation, he was able to make his way to the president.

Talent spoke first, "Yes, Jack, how did you like the meeting?"

Jack was afraid his lips would tremble. A little breathlessly, he responded, "I'm bothered by the listing of my committee. Who is the Johnson shown on it, and when do we get together to fill it out?"

"You don't know Greta! Very personable and intelligent. Should make an excellent member. The committee will be effective and efficient as it stands. I see no need to change it," Talent replied while turning to other members who were pressing for his attention.

Medford was confused; he couldn't think clearly. He didn't know where his thinking should begin. Everything seemed to be wrong at once.

"Jack Medford," said a voice behind him. He turned to see an attractive, late thirty's lady with a lively face. "I'm Greta Johnson, I don't believe we've met. The Board elected me at its May meeting last spring, just in time for me to attend the annual meeting in June. I have been assigned to your committee."

"Thank you for introducing yourself," he replied. With that, he was at a loss to continue. To talk about the committee was impossible. He was too ashamed of it, and of how it came about. But suddenly the significance dawned on him of her few weeks of membership, omitting the summer months, for a Board member assigned to the committee that handles personnel matters. It was yet another travesty. He decided to learn more. He asked, "Were you informed of your assignment?"

"Oh yes. Mr. Talent called me several weeks ago. We had talked briefly at the annual meeting when he wanted to know about my work experience. I thought he would be disappointed because I really don't have much. That is, I mean . . . , I sort of went from college into marriage and raising a family. I only had some hourly experience, but he didn't seem to mind."

Medford was beside himself, "I'm afraid I have to leave promptly. I have your addresses from the membership list. I'll be in touch with you. Good-by." As there was no one else he dared to speak with, he quickly found his way out of the room and out of the building.

RESOLUTION

Medford had trouble getting to bed that night. His humiliation wore on him as he paced up and down reviewing the evening's events. He considered, "To place a new Board member on the committee that handles personnel matters was unscrupulous. Johnson most likely has not yet connected the faces around the circle with the names on the roster. She is necessarily ignorant of what members have done and how they have performed. She will not be able to participate meaningfully in the deliberations of my committee. Apparently, the first year of her three year term of appointment will be wasted.

"Then there was Bob's declaration that no changes are needed in the committee: no immediate past president, no members with personnel experience, no long-timers who know everybody, no one but Greta Johnson. This is perverse.

"Could it be that her appointment was window dressing? That she was selected only to mollify the Board? It is monstrous.

"What am I up against?

"But rather, Who am I up against?" he continued. "What kind of a person is he? What does he intend? Weeks ago he gave Johnson her assignment. During these weeks, he refused to meet with me. But, actually, he didn't refuse; he never refused. It was only by his indirection that we never got together.

"So, it looks like he plans to have the governance committee for himself. He will leave no room for me."

In this way, during the next few days, Medford resolved these events. As he thought over what had happened since his election in June, he calculated that it added up quite nicely. The pieces fit together. He had been put in a box, and a rather small one at that. His mortification was complete.

"What am I to do?" Medford thought. "Take it to the Board? Take what? Ask the Board to decide how many appointees there ought to be on a committee and do so by voting on resolutions? Absurd. Complain to the Board about how I am being treated? That would appear as a personality clash, leading nowhere. Talk to my Board friends about it? Sure, have them over for a beer and lay out a picture of the stone wall I have run into. But to what end, to what purpose? Stand before the Board and persuade them that the president is misbehaving? I cannot handle that. He has done nothing wrong — nothing illicit, and I have no word or transgression to bring against him. I cannot quote a single phrase that can be held against him.

"As a committee chair with essentially no committee, I can do nothing through or with it. The bylaws do not mention a quorum for standing committees. I can call a meeting, but if Bob chooses not to show, what can I do with Johnson? She won't know the people we are talking about. If he does show, it will be me versus him, and we have seen how that works. I can endorse whatever Bob wants, but I cannot expect him to respond to what interests me. It is clear that he won't be listening to what I have to say, since he has avoided doing so from our election.

"For the year ahead, the committee certainly can go forward as it is now formed. As chair I would be subordinated to the president. I would be doing what he asks me to do, without regard to the purpose of the office. The chair of the GC is separately elected so as to be a check on the president, but how can I do that without a committee to validate my concerns? I would be a single voice perpetually complaining about procedural matters, and that would soon become tiresome," he concluded. "I have never been a flunky, and I would be unsuccessful trying to be one. I cannot hold up my head as chair of the present committee for the coming year."

After two days of agony, on Friday morning, Medford dispatched an e-mail message to Talent: Dear Bob, I herewith resign my elected position as chair of the governance committee effective immediately, (Signed) Jack Medford.

After he had sent the missive, his feeling of relief was palpable. Now he could view the world through fresh eyes. He hoped the humiliation that had engulfed him would evaporate quickly. To questions from Board members, the explanation for his resignation would be "policy disagreements." That should bring the unpleasantness to an end.

As for his continued participation on the Board, Medford would do that which was asked of him, so long as there were no political games to be played. He was pleased to have been selected by the previous GC to be an officer. He wished it could have worked out better than it did, but he was glad to be out of the grinder. With his resignation sent, the consternation was put to rest.

Or, so Jack Medford thought.

The following Monday evening, about seven o'clock, as the family was clearing the dining table, he received an unexpected phone call. It was from the Board president.

"Good evening, Jack," Talent said, "you surprised me with your resignation."

"Under the circumstances, I felt it was the right thing to do."

1. The First Two Steps

"If you choose to see it that way . . . I accept your decision and your resignation."

After a pause, Talent continued, "It does raise a difficulty however."

"How's that?" Jack answered brightly, but the pause that followed sickened him. He thought, "What possible difficulty could there be now that I am just an ordinary member of the Board like the others?"

Talent spelled out the difficulty. "It is impossible to ask you to chair a committee after you have just abandoned one. Even appointing you as a committee member raises the question of your level of commitment, and certainly there could be no consideration of appointment to a special or ad hoc assignment. I question if there is anything I can do with you."

"I see. I didn't think there would be a problem. I'll have to give it some thought."

"You do that. I'll keep in touch. Good night, Jack." With that, the president hung up.

". . . abandoned one!" he said aloud to himself.

"It can't be," he insisted. "It can't happen. Not more argument. Will it never end?"

By the next morning, Medford had adjusted his thoughts to the idea that the assault continued apace. He was able to ask himself, "What do I do now?"

He was pleased to see that this time he had an answer. "I will participate without a committee assignment. I won't be the only one. There are a couple of old codgers on board who continue without assignment, although each does have a singular purpose for his place on the Board." He imagined, "I'll enjoy the meetings, and participate in Board discussion, and I still have a vote. That will do it, and I'll see how the year goes along."

Tuesday evening, to Medford's astonishment, at six thirty, during dinner, there came a second phone call.

"I hope you realize, Jack," said Talent, "the impossible spot you have put me in with your peremptory resignation. The governance committee cannot function until I find a new chair. Furthermore, what am I to do with you? You really have done the Board an injury."

"Well, I'm sorry about that," said Jack. He attempted a defense: "If you will remember, I did have difficulty reaching you."

"There are always reasons, Jack, and as it happened things turned out just fine in the end. You were a little nervous in your new position, that's all there is to it. I'll continue to be in touch with you until this matter is settled. Good night." The president hung up.

"... peremptory resignation, ... done the Board an injury," Medford continued to be amazed at Talent's gratuitous aggression. He had never seen anything like it. "Will my phone ring tomorrow, on Wednesday evening? And if it does, how will I defend myself, having failed to do so this far?"

During Wednesday evening he could not take his mind off the telephone. As it didn't ring, the evening ran very late. "I can't live like this," thought Medford. "Am I to be terrorized by Talent and the telephone all week?"

On Thursday evening it rang again.

"I am exhausted by your behavior, Jack," said Talent in a hard voice. "There is nothing I can do with you."

But Jack was ready for this argument. He declared, "Just let me be a member without assignment. And for Heaven's sake stop calling me."

"It's my job to call you until I clear up the status of your assignment on the Board. There are twenty positions on the Board. We have a lot of work to do. You are asking to hold an idle seat."

"An idle seat?"

"If I cannot give you an assignment, your place on the Board is not contributing. It's as simple as that, Jack. I'll stay in touch. Good Night." The president hung up.

The drumbeat of conflict was too much. Medford was overwhelmed with an acute awareness that there could be no peace. His earlier feeling of humiliation had evaporated leaving behind plain, helpless anger.

"How did it happen that someone, anyone, on the Board dislikes me enough to want to get rid of me? I think Bob is wrong about needing the seat, but what can I do?" he meditated. "If I were to look to the Board for succor, there is no GC to which I could bring a complaint. I can't stand up before the assembled Board and lecture them as a way to show wrongdoing. And yet again, maybe he's right. Maybe in my special position, I'm of no use to the Board. In any case, I cannot continue with the harassment."

There was no call on Friday. Saturday morning he sent a second e-mail message: Dear Bob, I herewith resign from the Board of Trustees effective immediately, (Signed) Jack Medford.

The following Monday evening, the president called at eight to accept his resignation, to thank him for it, and to mention that in December it is the Board's practice to hold a reception for present and former Board members. "I hope to see you there, Jack," he said, and with that he closed the call.

The president was pleased. As he put down the phone, he thought to himself, "A Board of Trustees . . . , caught and leashed. The policeman is gone. No witnesses remain. And, best of all, I have his replacement at hand."

Note 1: End of Collegiality

Collegiality evaporates from the Board with the election of this new president. While it continues with individual members, of course, it disappears from the Board as a normative mode of behavior. An "us" versus "them" mode of operation, led by the new president, takes its place.

Jack Medford became a "them" immediately upon election because Talent, much earlier, had made a carefully honed assessment. After Medford's selection for nomination, the president estimated that his innate initiative and sense of responsibility would be a threat to the president's plans. The president would have to remove him from office as the first order of business.

In this chapter, the newly constituted governance committee comes into being almost as though Medford did not exist. When Medford responds by resigning from the GC, he hears himself accused of having "abandoned" his post, as though his reasons were personal. In this manipulation, the president allows no room for comity. The president overwhelmed Jack Medford by acting toward him first with pervasive reticence, and then with intense aggression. In that way Talent accomplished his first purpose.

This action leaves Robert Talent entirely free to behave as he will without a "policeman" available to watch him or to be called upon by what will become other "them" members.

Because this treatment of Medford is shameful, the Board must remain unaware of it. The Board thus gets divided into the small "us" contingent who accept that behavior, and the "them" members who suffer it. This lack of collegiality will bring about a dormant, silent Board, and matters of governance will get arranged outside the Board's awareness.

Those who become members of the "them" contingent should respond as follows: do not resign from either office or membership. Suffer the insults to prevent turnover of office positions. Hold on to where you are until there comes forth a better day.

The other technique, illustrated in this first chapter by the Greta Johnson appointment, fills important positions, such as membership on the GC, with weak individuals, thus holding those positions filled and therefore unavailable for more capable persons.

2. Getting Acquainted

FIRST CONFERENCE

Anthony Petrillo came from the horse ranch operation. He was an expert rider and had won a number of awards in national competitions. He had married young, his wife teaching in the Academy, their two children attending the high school, and the family residing in a house on the campus. He rose over the years to become manager of the riding school, and during this time acquired a BA degree in American history from Bidwell, a nearby liberal arts college that was of considerable repute in the northwest. More than a decade ago, during a reorganization of the Academy structure, his position as manager of the riding school was attached to the headmaster's office as assistant headmaster, a position he held for a number of years, while, at the same time, carrying a teaching assignment in the history department, which he later chaired. In due course, the Board had selected him for headmaster.

Shortly after the election of officers in June, the new president joined with the Academy's headmaster at a luncheon consisting solely of fine food and fine pleasantries. With the summer vacation time upon them, and at the president's suggestion, they agreed to meet at 4:00 p.m. on the first Friday after the resumption of classes in September.

Like most summers, it flew by altogether too quickly.

That hour of the first Friday soon arrived. As Robert Talent approached the familiar open counter of the school's administrative office area, the headmaster's secretary greeted him, "Mr. Talent, welcome. Tony will be with you in a moment. Did you have a good summer?"

"Very good, Claire. It was fine, although it went by altogether too quickly," replied the president. "By the way, while we're in conference, can you intercept phone calls for us? We have much to do."

"Of course."

He continued, "And no coffee, please?"

"As you wish."

While she was speaking, the headmaster's office door swung open. Petrillo strode out and offered his hand to Talent. "It's so good to see you. I trust your summer was enjoyable. Come in, please."

He led the way in. He led the way toward his desk set diagonally in the far corner facing the center of the office, where there were a couple of arm chairs that matched the desk.

After closing the door firmly behind him, Talent stood at a conference table that was set near the wall where they had entered. "I would prefer, Tony," said Talent, "to sit at your conference table over here. Would that be possible this afternoon?"

Caught quite off guard, Petrillo jerked to a halt. He said, "Of course, wherever you like." Actually, he did not appreciate leaving the comfort of having his big desk in front of him and a tight room corner behind his back. He sat down at the conference table directly across from the president, who sat straight up against the table edge.

Petrillo continued, "I can honestly say, Bob, that the school — its academics, arts, athletics, everything — came right up to speed in the first week," while he felt that he was placed somewhat too close to the president's face.

"I have always thought of you, Tony, as an excellent administrator," Talent said. "When you were slipped in as headmaster by Richards eight years ago, from your previous position as assistant headmaster, the school was in dire budgetary straits. One might even allow its survival could be questioned. But you straightened things out quickly. We owe you a debt of gratitude for that."

Petrillo took a deep breath. This was not going to be easy. He started, "Money was being handled loosely. The many copiers we had all over the place were eating us alive. We got rid of all but two. And we tightened the budgeting process."

He continued, "But my appointment, Bob, was entirely according to rule and procedure."

"Of course it was, Tony," said Talent, "I was just referring to the way Richards suddenly asked the executive committee to confirm you as the sole nominee, and called a special session of the Board to confirm your appointment. As you know, no placement search was ever made; no advertisement was ever placed; no interviews were ever held. That's all I was referring to, Tony, nothing more."

"That was Richard's doing; that's how he wanted to handle it."

"Well, it worked out for the best, didn't it?"

"Yes," Petrillo finished, "I think it worked out well for the school."

2. Getting Acquainted

Talent, his first topic having gone smoothly, moved his agenda to the next item.

"Along with the assistant's job, Tony, as I understand the history of this place, you were the chair of the History Department."

"I majored in history at Bidwell College."

"And you were a riding star, if I am not mistaken?"

"I won the Northwest competition in my last year there," Petrillo replied.

"You came from the ranch and from teaching history," Talent continued. "But we seem to have had trouble lately moving the riding team into the winner's circle. Now Elbert manages riding. How are we going to do this year?"

"It's in great form. Elbert has had three years to build it up. We have a good chance for the Class A competition."

"And Board member Frederick Jacobs," said Talent, changing the subject. "I have heard he was your roommate at Bidwell."

"He was my riding teammate and roommate. So we have known each other for many, many years. I hope you don't object to his presence on the Board."

"Certainly not. But be sure to let me know beforehand if something comes up on that score. I don't tolerate surprises very well.

"Do you know, Tony, the reason I am here at the Academy? My son was always a good rider, and he wanted to go to a school that had its own stables. Otherwise, we would have found ourselves at that new academy on the north side of the city. That place would have been much more compatible to me and my family."

"Is that so? What did you find about this place, Bob, that was, may I ask, incompatible?"

"Oh Tony! It's hidebound; nothing has changed in forty years. But maybe we can do something about that in due course."

Talent thought, "Done with that. . . ."

He paused for a moment to judge the atmosphere. He decided that there was plenty of room for one more hard push.

"Tony, from my several years of association with the Academy and my time on the Board, I perceive that there is yet some considerable angst remaining among the faculty concerning your appointment."

"Not a bit," replied the headmaster in a too-quick and too-loud voice. "Those feelings were gone years ago. Indeed Bob, there were a few complainers, but they have quieted down."

"So you say," responded Talent, "but you seem to be somewhat afraid of the faculty. I notice you only meet with the whole body of the faculty in Anderson Hall, or you meet with individual members singly in your office. Nothing else."

"What's your concern, Bob? What you're referring to, I see as efficiency." Petrillo pushed back, "Are you collecting rumors about me?"

"Not at all," replied Talent. "I would never do that. In fact, I approve of your appointment last year of Wilson from the history department as chairman of the faculty. I think he should serve your purposes well. As a matter of fact, I consider you to be an excellent headmaster, and I look forward to our having a constructive working relationship. I suggest that we meet at this time each Friday afternoon. Is that okay with you?"

"Yes. Of course. I would be glad to do that," said Petrillo, keenly aware that he could say nothing else. He hoped they were getting near to the end of the meeting.

Talent kept his agenda moving along.

"Something will be coming up this fall that needs our special attention, Tony," added Talent. "You know the Langmuir boy in the ninth grade?"

Petrillo was relieved. He was glad to get back to a topic where he had some authority. He replied, "Oh yes. He's been with us since the sixth grade, and he's an excellent student."

"His mother," continued Talent, "is a corporate lawyer with Englemark where they make jet engines, and his father, Creston, has a Ph.D. from Harvard in philosophy. Needless to say, they are a well-spoken couple. It seems Creston is, as you might expect, a bookish or academic type of person who likes to chat with faculty members about their specialties. He'll ask the chair of the mathematics department in what grade do they start calculus, and when do they get to vector addition. The faculty just loves it, Tony."

"We get that kind of parent from time to time," said the headmaster, "maybe he would be helpful on the Board."

"Exactly. And that's the problem. As a member of the Board, wouldn't he be something of a threat to you?"

Talent waited to let that last phrase sink in.

Finally Petrillo said, "Oh . . . Yes . . . I see . . ."

"There are voices ready to promote Langmuir as a Board candidate. Unfortunately, under these circumstances, we can't refuse him a seat. He is too well known and liked by too many of the faculty and parents. So he will come on the Board, probably at our November meeting."

For the first time, Petrillo's voice took on a compliant tone, "Is there anything I can do?"

"Yes, Tony, there is. It comes immediately after he is voted onto the Board. You approach him and ask him to undertake some volunteer project for the school; something he can work on; it should be substantial, not just

2. Getting Acquainted

make-work. He's retired. He has lots of free time. Give him something meaty to do. Preferably alone."

"For years I have wanted a study done of our use of the busses. They are expensive, and they put an additional burden on the faculty who have to drive them. Maybe he could do that?" suggested Petrillo with some enthusiasm.

"Just what the doctor ordered, Tony. But remember, it must be offered after the Board vote, and immediately so."

Petrillo thought, "Not bad. I can work with this guy. It's not pleasant with him right in my face — I can smell his breath. But, all in all, it's doable."

While Petrillo enjoyed his brief reverie, Talent lined up his final topics.

"That bulletin we get from the Association of Private Schools, Tony," said Talent. "That school in Monterey that is looking for a new headmaster. They had eighty-three applications, if you can believe it. Are there really that many headmasters out on the street?"

"That's a pretty nice school, Bob," responded Petrillo. "Many applications will come from safely established headmasters who are looking for more prestige and money."

"I understand that the average tenure of a headmaster is about eight years?"

"That's right," said Petrillo, only realizing afterwards that eight years was his own time where he was sitting. He thought, "What in hell is this guy going for next?"

Talent was hard at work: "By the way, how come this school does not yet have a sexuality education course?"

This was old ground for Petrillo. "The faculty objects. They complain that such courses are always out of control. Nobody can find out what they are actually teaching — what actually goes on in the classroom. So they always refuse."

But Talent was purposeful: "What if you bring in someone and, instead of having them report to the faculty, simply have the new teacher report directly to you?"

Petrillo was flabbergasted, "Can I get away with that?"

"The Board will have nothing to say on the matter. I'll get a name for you to interview."

Talent considered himself now to be well established in the headmaster's office. He offered, "Let's wrap up this meeting, shall we?"

Petrillo was relieved. "I have nothing more," he said.

But Talent did. "I would ask you and your accountant, Goodacre, to please be as responsive as possible to the new chair of the Board's budget committee. Pierre de Vanough has wide experience running an operation about the size of this school. I have the utmost confidence in him. I think you will find him most capable."

"Certainly."

"Shall we adjourn?"

Petrillo was thankful, "That does it for me."

As the president left, Petrillo made a mental note to look about the school for a wider conference table.

Note 2: Intimidation

We have here nothing less than intimidation and, with it, subjugation. By making reference to the headmaster's professional vulnerabilities, the president makes clear that the headmaster's livelihood is the consideration in their relationship.

After bringing up, one by one, the headmaster's shortcomings, the new president says to him: "In fact, I consider you an excellent headmaster, and I look forward to our having a constructive working relationship. I suggest that we meet at this time each Friday afternoon. Is that okay with you?" Clearly, Petrillo will be "an excellent headmaster" only if he accepts the president's suggestions at their meetings, which will occur, he learns, frequently. The headmaster's acquiescence greatly compromises his authority.

This dialog establishes a degenerate professional relationship in which the president has extortionate influence over the headmaster's actions as manager of the school. This will permit the president's policy initiatives to appear to the world as though they were the headmaster's administrative decisions. As we learned in chapter one, the president, in accomplishing this subordination, will have used no sentence that can be quoted against him.

Only the chair of the governance committee can deal with this delicate subordination. He must use his position as an elected officer, where he is on a par with the president. Informal but sensitive conversations with the headmaster and senior staff should suffice to sniff out the bad relationship imposed by the president, and the considerable burden of frequent meetings. Such sniffing out must be accomplished without expecting the headmaster to offer testimony against a member of the Board. The chairman must persuade his committee members of the problem, presumably over the president's objections.

These two chapters illustrate how takeover activities use two principal venues for action: the telephone call between two people, and non-committee meetings of two persons. Very little is done in the organized committee and plenum meetings.

3. The Replacement

A JOB OFFER

John Stoddart, a long time executive for a no longer extant Seattle coffee importing company, moved to this area upon retirement. This fall he began his ninth year serving on the Academy's Board, although never as an officer or even committee chairman. A three-piece suit patrician, he stood tall and erect, every aspect announcing authority, except that in conversation he might be perceived as a little slow on the uptake.

In late October, shortly before the November Board meeting, he received a phone call from president Talent.

"John, how are you, and how is Betsy?"

"We're just fine, thank you, Bob," Stoddart responded. "We had a hectic summer with numerous guests, and we're glad it's fall. How are you and Janice doing, and how are things going with your new position on the Board? I thought the October meeting went well."

"As a matter of fact, John, that's what I'm calling about. I had plans for a strong management team, and they have been blown asunder. Last week Jack Medford suddenly resigned from the Board. What do you make of that kind of behavior?" he asked.

"That's terrible. We were depending on him. I gather he has completely let us down?"

"Very much so. I take you to be a reliable fellow with serious executive experience. Could you see fit to join my management team?"

"I'll do anything I can to help," John offered. "What would you like me to do?"

"I would like you to stand for election as chair of the governance committee."

John replied, "I would be pleased to do so."

"We will make a great team, I believe, John. We'll get together soon after the election and I'll outline our plans for the year. I will look for and need your support to move them along."

John's response was firm, "Bob, you can count on my full support in whatever you undertake."

"Thank you, John. I'll set up the election for the November meeting. You don't mind that it is too late to get it included on the published agenda?"

"Not at all," John replied.

Talent went to his next subject, "We have two new members coming on the Board. I would like to move them along quickly. They are Elaine Rutherford Blandley and Creston Langmuir."

"How have they been sponsored?"

"I am sponsoring Blandley. She is a most intelligent person with good experience in getting things done effectively on trustee Boards. The other, Langmuir, has been promoted for the Board by senior members of the faculty," Bob explained.

John replied, "Sounds good. I would have no objection to either one."

Talent continued, "Fine, John, that's how I like to work. I think we can get a lot done together in the year ahead. I have also cleared these two names with Greta Johnson. After your election, I will offer them to the Board for election. Is that all right with you?"

"Yes, of course."

"Thank you very much, John. I'll see you at the November meeting," said Talent, as he closed the call.

A GATHERING

Talent was pleased with Stoddart. He would be easy to work with and safe. And now, with the school year well underway, he had much to engender.

During the years prior to his own election as president, he had successfully, if somewhat furtively, sponsored two friends for membership on the Board. Pierre de Vanough manages a small and prosperous manufacturing firm of several dozen employees. Talent had worked with him previously on a non-profit Board of Directors where they came to appreciate each other's operational craftsmanship. Ruth Blanchard was a lady of some leisure in her mid-forties, and experienced at Board activism. She loved the challenge, and agreed immediately to help. Both agreed to help Talent accomplish the changes he wanted to make. Neither were otherwise associated with the Academy, but Talent had introduced them to the

3. The Replacement

chair of the GC as specialists, each of whom would be able to make a significant contribution to the work of the Board. They had been members now for almost two years. The president e-mailed them invitations to a meeting at his home one evening during the following week, but gave them arrival times fifteen minutes apart.

Talent was well aware that he had snubbed the previous president, Papalian, by not offering him an appointment to the GC, as was usually done. The considerable turnover of membership from the previous year left him as the only member who knew of Talent's connection to De Vanough and Blanchard. Papalian was ensconced on the buildings and grounds committee and, as long as he remained quiet, the president would tolerate his presence on the Board.

Robert Talent maintained his old house and its grounds impeccably. The three of them met in the kind of room once called a sun parlor. It was connected off the south side of the living room and had windows around three sides. It being evening, the shades were drawn. His wife, Janice, brought in dessert-like refreshments with tea and coffee, and left, closing the door behind her. She understood that the two visitors, whom she had met before, were members of the Academy Board, and that interruptions from the children or telephone were to be avoided. With the door closed and television playing in the living room, the meeting achieved complete privacy.

Talent opened the meeting with some good news. "First, I am pleased to tell you that I have in hand Jack Medford's resignation."

"Wonderful," said de Vanough. "I don't know how you do it, Bob, but without that, we could never fix the place."

"It will be announced at the November meeting."

"Do you want one of us to take his place?"

"No, that won't be necessary. I have already found a perfect replacement, John Stoddart. Well . . . , I have his agreement to be chair of the GC. He will have to be elected at the meeting. He is extraordinarily presentable, but utterly without imagination or initiative, which explains why he was kept on the Board for these many years, but never given anything to do.

"The two of us will be a management team, running the Board effectively and efficiently, just like the trustee handbooks say we should."

"John . . . ?" asked Blanchard, "He's a retired executive. What if he decides at some point that he doesn't like what you are doing? What if he doesn't like your weekly meetings with the headmaster?"

"Yes," answered Talent, "he once had an executive title, but he was a salesman. You know how banks make their sales people into so many vice-presidents? Well, other firms do that too. At the same time he will be useful; he will be diligent and competent in doing whatever I ask of him. So I expect, Ruth, we have nothing to worry about. I will engage some member to offer his nomination.

"However, there are some other things we have to worry about. We may have to remove as many as three more members. Our purpose, as always, needs a quiet Board. We can't have people suddenly offering resolutions or trying to lead the Board rhetorically by making speeches.

So, I am bringing another helper on board for us, Elaine Rutherford Blandley, the wife of the president of Bidwell College. She is well versed in the methods I use. I gather that their Board is managed somewhat as we are doing here, when necessary. This kind of action is much more widespread than one might ordinarily assume.

"One of our worries is Creston Langmuir, an academic type of person. The faculty loves him, so we had to let him at least come on the board. I'm setting him up with a give and take exercise. So Pierre, I'll need you to sit beside him at the December meeting."

"I'll be there."

"I have Board quieting well underway," continued Talent. "No one seems to notice, so far, that we do not read or distribute minutes of the previous meeting. We had no committee reports in October. There was only one complaint, and that faded quickly. We'll see how things go in November and December.

"I've had a long chat with Tony Petrillo. The first purposeful talk we've had. He gives every indication of understanding the new situation and cooperating fully, but we will have to watch him. I plan to have meetings with him each Friday at 4:00 p.m. They will run a half hour at least, and possibly an hour. That's where I will get our work done.

"Tony and I have avoided the faculty objections to adding a sexuality course by having the teacher report directly to him instead of the faculty. Elaine Blandley knows a teacher who is tough enough to open the door on that subject at the Academy. You, Pierre, in your office as chair of the budget committee, will work with the bookkeeper to find and move the funds to pay her."

De Vanough did not see a problem. "The bookkeeper is on my committee, as you know. But if I go over the change with him beforehand, so that he has an opportunity to clear it with Tony, he will say nothing. I'm not sure my committee members will even notice how the numbers change. I do have one nitpicker on board, but I can gloss it over if anyone comments."

Talent advanced his agenda, "Ruth, at the November meeting I would like to assign the development of a long range plan for the school to you."

"Oh, dear," exclaimed Ruth, "I'm not very good at writing reports."

3. The Replacement

"If you will collect the data," answered Talent, "I will find someone to write the report for submission. If there is an objection that the assignment must be made to a committee not to an individual – we have not yet quieted the Board completely – just stand mute. Say nothing, okay?"

"Yes."

"Unless you have questions, that concludes our work for the evening," said Talent. "Remember, some people are good at constructing a social map of a group like the Board. Please keep in mind that we are never seen exchanging papers, walking, sitting, talking, ever, anywhere together. When talking with other members, be careful in conversation to make no inadvertent reference to contacts between us.

"I thank you both for the help you are giving me; it is much appreciated."

With that, he closed the meeting. The two visited briefly with the family in the living room, and left separately. Talent was well pleased. His year as president was set in place.

NOVEMBER

The November Board of Trustees meeting took place in the evening in a private room at a local restaurant. Coffee, tea, soft drinks, and some munchy treats were available on a side table.

President Talent opened the meeting with an expression of greetings to everyone, and a note of appreciation for their attendance that evening. He welcomed their two invited guests, the headmaster of the school, and a senior faculty member slated to become head of the anticipated, to be newly formed, middle school. Although there was a third guest present, he was not introduced at this time.

Talent began the meeting by expressing his sorrow at having to announce the resignation of the chair of the governance committee, Jack Medford, from the Board.

Talent continued in a subdued voice with an item not listed on the published agenda, "We will have to elect a replacement." And after a pause, "The floor is opened to nominations for chair of the governance committee."

One of the members raised her hand and received a nod from the president. "I nominate John Stoddart for chairman of the governance committee," she announced in a stately voice.

"Are there further nominations?" asked Talent, who waited seven seconds. "If there are none, nominations are closed."

Again, after a pause, he said, "We will now hold the vote. All those in favor of John Stoddart for chair of the governance committee please raise your hand." Most members voted. After a pause, he went on, "All those opposed." No hands were raised. He announced, "John Stoddart is elected chair of the committee. I want to thank the Board for giving us a new chair of this important committee so promptly."

The president moved ahead, "The election of a chair for the committee allows us to proceed with the election of two new Board candidates. They have been accepted by the GC, and the new chair has given his assent also. We consider them to be fully qualified for membership, and we recommend them to the Board."

"I give you Elaine Rutherford Blandley," he announced. "You have received her completed questionnaire showing her background and qualifications. Are we ready for a vote?"

There was no response. After a pause, Talent asked, "Please raise your hand for a vote of aye." Most, if not all, raised their hand. "Those opposed?" No hands were raised. "Ms. Blandley is admitted to membership on the Board for a term of three years."

Talent went through the same process with the candidacy of Creston Langmuir, and accomplished the same result.

Addressing the assembly, he explained that, "I invited our two candidates, if they wished to do so, to wait for the vote in the restaurant. They both took me up on the invitation. Would the secretary invite them in please, so they can join us?"

When they came in, Talent offered them his congratulations, welcomed them, and introduced them to the Board. He then turned promptly to the continuing agenda.

"As you are aware," said the president to open a new item, "the school is giving consideration to gathering three grades – six, seven, and eight – into an administratively separate middle school. This change will require the attention and approval of the Board. In fact, it is of sufficient importance that it will be done in two steps. We will have a vote today to show tentative approval. During the next several months you will have opportunity to learn more about the change before a second, and governing, vote next February. I would like to ask Tony if he would be so kind as to walk us through the plans."

The headmaster spoke to the assembly for about five minutes, took several routine questions about details, and finished with a summary.

3. The Replacement

The president took over, "Let's have a show of hands of those who would favor this change." Most hands went up. "Those opposed?" No hands were raised. "Thank you very much, and thank you Tony for your help."

Talent's third guest had been sitting with the Board for an hour. He had saved this item for the end of the meeting to reduce the opportunity for questions. Now he continued.

"The Board has hired a consultant to help it in matters that will be coming before it. Let me introduce Talbot Train of Train Associates. Talbot has been consulting with nonprofit groups, including private schools, for more than a decade, and comes to us well recommended.

"Talbot would you tell us, please, about yourself and your organization?"

Train spoke up in a clear, well modulated voice, "I have been helping nonprofit organizations and, in particular, independent secondary schools, for more than ten years. My areas of experience are cost control, staff assessment and search, development planning, and organization structure analysis. I will be pleased to help the Board and the Academy in areas of my experience. My rate of reimbursement is seven hundred and fifty dollars per day. Thank you."

"Thank you Talbot."

That item completed Talent's agenda.

Miscellaneous announcements and event promotions took another thirty minutes. After which, Talent thanked them, reminded them of the December date for their next meeting, and adjourned the assembly.

Note 3: A Confederacy

For our protagonist to achieve 100 percent influence over the Board's actions, which is his immediate objective, he will need helpers. Together they constitute a confederacy within the Board. It is unlikely that the president would find willing and able helpers already in place on the Board. He will bring them on board, and thus create for himself critical vulnerabilities. Once these confederates are in place as members of the Board, they must avoid showing connections among themselves. He warns his helpers, "Remember, some people are good at constructing a social map of a group."

Bringing helpers onto the Board requires great care. Talent, during his time before becoming president, brought two new members to the Board. Talent "had successfully, if furtively, sponsored two friends for membership on the Board." They necessarily will be friends of the protagonist and may have served with him on other Boards. Only in this way can he know what covert actions he can ask of them. It is likely they will have had no other association with the Academy: "Neither of them was otherwise associated with the Academy, but Talent had introduced them to the then chair of the governance committee as specialists of one sort or another." The helpers do not direct their allegiance to the academy, as do the other members; it goes to the protagonist instead.

To accomplish a takeover, the protagonist has to establish and maintain a silent Board: "We may have to remove as many as three more members if we are to quiet the Board sufficiently. Our purpose, as always, needs a quiet Board. We can't have people suddenly offering resolutions or trying to lead the Board rhetorically by making speeches." That's right. Sudden resignations become a sign that a takeover is underway, as does an obviously silent Board. A takeover that is underway exposes members to the possibility of rough treatment. Candidates for this treatment will be those who raise questions, who wonder aloud that the Board operates in a strange manner, who spontaneously place resolutions on the floor, who on their own initiative address the Board, or who ask for a reading of the minutes. Keep an eye on what happens to them.

4. A Setup

THE BUSSING STUDY

As the November Board meeting broke up, Tony Petrillo caught up with Creston Langmuir.

"Creston, I want to ask you something," he said, speaking closely to him. "I'm looking for a volunteer to do a study for the school. Could I interest you in something of that sort?"

"You probably can, Tony. I'm a study-ish sort of person," Creston replied. "What's up?"

"Well, we have a serious bussing problem here at the Academy," Petrillo explained. "We use busses to bring and take students each day over quite a wide area at a considerable expense, and at an enormous imposition on the teaching staff who do the driving. As you know, we also use the busses to truck the various sports teams about with their equipment from school to school.

"Would you consider doing a study of the costs and needs of our bussing system?"

Langmuir was interested. "As you know, I'm retired, so I do have time available," he replied. "I have a background for something like that and could do it quite straightforwardly. How soon do you need it done?"

"It's been a long time waiting to get done, so I can't say there is a deadline. I suppose it would take several months?"

"That sounds reasonable. I'll tuck into it, if you wish, and keep you informed of my progress."

"Thank you very much, Creston. I'll look forward to hearing from you," Petrillo replied, and took his leave.

MAKING A CONTRIBUTION

Langmuir was pleased. "It's the kind of study I know exactly how to do. It obviously is important for the school.

"Another difficulty that surely is on Tony's mind is the matter of faculty recruitment. It suffers from the requirement laid on new teachers that, in addition to their many other obligations, they were to get up early to drive a bus for an hour, and drive again after school. Such a schedule is a tough sell. It leads to teacher turnover."

Langmuir did tuck in. He drove the busses to see what condition they were in and pumped the teacher that managed their maintenance. He found the available use and cost data, and gathered it up for his report. He would file an early report with that data graphed out, see what Petrillo thought about it and talk with Mrs. Snow, then submit a final report with conclusions and recommendations.

"I have to worry about the opinion of Mrs. Snow," Langmuir thought concerning the long-time director of admissions. "How would a curtailing of student bussing to and from the school affect admissions? There could be no curtailment without her acceptance."

It occurred to Langmuir that there might be, in this assignment, a hidden purpose. "Maybe she and Petrillo had reached a standoff about the value and burden of the bussing program, and it is now my job to reconcile the two with a policy recommendation supported by data.

"I will have to interview Snow carefully to smoke out what is going on," he realized.

Within ten days, Langmuir had pulled together his cost and usage data. He wrapped up his preliminary report of the data, signed it, and left it with Claire in the headmaster's office.

"I put in a good many hours on it," Langmuir mused. "But I think I have made a good job of it. In the next month or so, I'll complete the final report. I'll limn the arguments for a reduction to take place during the next school year. I will, of course, go over that in detail with Mrs. Snow, and submit the final report before Christmas vacation."

Fortunately he was able to see her the following week and found that she was quite open-minded about the matter because enrollments were well up and included a substantial waiting list. They could take a small hit if that would be otherwise helpful for the school. Movement of the sports teams required busses and drivers; there was no alternative to that. But a careful presentation of the recommended change with its associated cost savings would have to wait for the final report.

4. A Setup

GETTING SERVED

As Friday afternoon approached, Tony Petrillo fretted about his coming meeting with the president. He had given a lot of thought to their first meeting. "It was," he concluded, "a great big push on me. Each of my injured sides was articulated in full, and then pushed aside for the moment. These aspects of my record would raise no problems with Bob as long as everything went smoothly. Well . . . so be it."

"The first meeting," he mused, "was to set the table. Now, I am about to get served. What will it be? I have no choice but to let him speak first."

The president showed up at his usual time.

Petrillo greeted him, "Good afternoon, Bob."

"Good afternoon, Tony."

Petrillo led Talent into his office.

As they went, Talent gave Claire a full face to face look, so she would remember that there were to be no interruptions.

Petrillo didn't dare suggest they sit across his desk. As they sat across the table, he was more than a little anxious.

Talent opened, "It appears that the new course on sexuality has been set up with a sufficient budget and suitable reporting arrangement."

"Yes, everything is arranged, except that I have to find a teacher. Because of faculty misgivings and parental concerns, the teacher will get a lot of buffeting."

"As I mentioned at our last meeting, Tony, I have a name and phone number for you. Here it is. She has done this before and can handle the gaff. She is also well credentialed. There should be no difficulties. Interview her, and let me know how it goes."

Petrillo thought, "My God, this guy does everything. He sure does want to get that course established." It occurred to the headmaster, "I wonder what else Bob plans to do with the curriculum? And he says that I am not to worry about reactions from the Board. Can he have each of the twenty members in a bind of some sort to keep them quiet? Is that done?"

Talent moved to the next item. "There are a few things I need help on, Tony," he continued. "The first concerns the two votes the Board is to take to formally establish the Middle School, of which we have had the first. It is your usual practice, is it not, to send out a letter to the Academy family at this time of year?"

"Yes. It's an upbeat letter to the parents, and everyone else, about how the year is going. I use it as an opportunity to treat subjects of which I want everyone to be aware."

"I have here," Talent responded, taking out a folded sheet of paper, "two sentences I want inserted near the end of your letter. They read as follows: As you know, the Board is taking two votes about the establishment of a middle school for grades six, seven, and eight. Of these two, it is the first vote that will govern the outcome.'"

Petrillo swooned, "What in hell is he doing now?" While keeping a quiet face, he thought, "He just told the Board that the second vote is to be the determining one. The first vote has already been taken at the November assembly. What is he getting me into?"

Talent noticed that this thrust required of Petrillo a real effort to digest it. The president watched, "His neck and face only colored slightly, and now he's breathing again. He seems to be coming around quickly."

Petrillo broached his problem gingerly, "What do you suggest I am to do with this if I get phone calls raising questions?"

"Say nothing," Talent responded. "Refer the matter to me, if you must. Whatever you do, Tony, don't try explaining things."

"How could I possibly explain these things?"

"Be sure to follow my text exactly; no elaboration."

"I understand," answered the headmaster. He was thinking, "I'll have to dodge at least a few inquiries about that one, but it can be done. I only wonder what's coming next. How many zingers can this guy throw at me in just one meeting? Maybe we're nearly done."

The president had yet two more items for him.

"As you are well aware, Tony, it is difficult for many families to meet tuition requirements at private schools. I would like the budget committee to consider including a premium in next years tuition rate to be used to aid those who otherwise cannot afford to come here."

"What would you like me to do?"

"If you would advise Goodacre that this topic will come up at the next budget committee meeting, Tony, that would be fine. I would like to have Pierre meet with him before then, so they can get some numbers ready. You and I both attend the budget meetings, so we will be there to participate. Let's see if it is not possible to do something about this problem."

"Okay, I'll be glad to tell him," said Petrillo. He was thinking, "The budget committee will be asked to make such an important decision? Has the Board gone away somewhere?"

4. A Setup

The president moved to his last topic.

"You mentioned the other day that you had a partial report from Langmuir. Could I see it, please?"

"Of course." Petrillo went to his desk and pulled it from a basket. "As we expected, it is concise, has in it the right info, and is professionally presented."

"Did he sign it?"

"Yes, as a matter of fact, he did sign it," reported Petrillo thumbing through the pages.

Talent made the quick judgement that Petrillo was sufficiently inculcated in his new role that he would accept a strong order. He said, "I want you to terminate the project immediately."

Petrillo sank into an emotional slough of helplessness. He thought, "How can I remain as headmaster and, at the same time, keep taking these hits. On the other hand, if I want to remain headmaster, I have to take these hits. Will this elitist monster across the table from me ever run out of secret motives?"

Petrillo's emotional slough did not last long. He pulled himself together sufficiently to ask, "Are you sure?" Recovering, he thought, "Uh-oh, I shouldn't have said that. I'm pretty well washed out trying to keep up a sensible dialog with this guy." Without waiting for a reply, he asked, "How will I present Creston with our decision?"

"Our decision," mused Talent, repeating to himself Petrillo's words."

"You say nothing," answered Talent. "He is a Board member. It will be most appropriate for me to inform him of it," said Talent, as he calculated that it was exactly thirteen days to the December Board meeting.

The president had run out of topics. After he took his leave, Tony was left alone. It pleased him to remember, "This morning, Claire told me the library had a conference table much like mine except that it was fourteen inches wider. I'll have to take a look at it."

A CONSULTATION

Pierre de Vanough liked to visit with Robert Talent, if only to talk shop. They had known each other for more than a decade. They had lots to gab about in addition to their present activity at the Academy. Talent had called him that morning to suggest lunch. It was convenient for them to hole up at the back of a short-order lunch spot in an old section of the city far from the Academy. He broke his own rule about them never being seen together in public, but they were careful enough to get away with it. In fact, if someone from the school were to come into the place, one of them would slip out through the kitchen into the alley, and walk away.

This meeting was about business. The new teacher to whom Blandley had referred them was scheduled for an interview with Petrillo shortly. If things went well, she would start next September with the school's first course on sexuality education for the eighth grade.

"Tony is pretty worried about the faculty and the Board, not to mention the parents," said Talent. "At her interview, she will inform Petrillo that the course will be mandatory for every student. It will be tough going at first. But I think the course will come through successfully."

De Vanough asked, "Do you want me to help in some way?"

"No. Just bringing you up to date.

"Where I will need your help, Pierre, is with Creston Langmuir at the December meeting. As you know, he's smart, so I rank him as something of a mortal enemy. He had to be admitted to the Board in the first place because he had much emotional support from the faculty. We just couldn't say no to him. We are using the give-and-take routine with him and hope it will work. Tony set him up with a volunteer activity for the school to study the bussing situation, its costs and needs. He has already turned in a preliminary, and thoroughly professional, report about the usage and expense statistics. Yesterday I informed Tony that the project was now terminated. He was disappointed, but he went along."

De Vanough interrupted, "Which of you gets to tell Langmuir of the termination?"

"Neither."

Talent explained, "About the Board meeting — it is twelve days away — at some point during it, I will bring up the bussing program. I will praise and thank Langmuir for his 'very professional report.' That's it, Pierre, only two sentences, with the second one ending with the word report.'"

De Vanough asked, "What about these next twelve days, though? What if he drops in to talk to Tony?"

"He doesn't seem to work that way, but it is a risk. I have in mind something to forestall that possibility. In the meantime, I need you to do what you do so well, Pierre. This item will not be on the published agenda, so it will be a complete surprise to Langmuir. He thinks what he is doing is a school project, and that the Board has nothing and should have nothing to do with it. Of course, technically speaking, he is right. He's smart, Pierre, but he's doing his thinking inside a small box.

4. A Setup

"At the meeting, sit beside Langmuir. I will state my two sentences praising the program, implying that it has been completed, and ending with the word report.' While Creston is still waiting for my next sentence, you go to work. Engage him in talk, controversial talk. In about seven seconds, I can move the Board to the next agenda item. After that, it will be too late for him to say anything. Hours later, after thinking about what happened, he will realize that the project is finished, that it is closed."

"Gotcha. No problem. But I'd like to have the full sentences beforehand. It helps my timing."

"I'll have them for you. Which brings up the next question – and not too early – Who will succeed me next June?"

"Why not set yourself up for a second term, Bob?"

"They don't do that here. It would be risky. People might start to ask too many questions. You are perfectly right that we do need three or four more years. We have the Board well on its way to being silent; I don't want to take a chance on upsetting what we have done so far."

Talent continued, "Take a careful look at Beth Perwick. She is a graduate of the Academy thirty years ago. She has been on the Board three years and is very presentable. She went from college into marriage and family. No work; no office politics. A little time with the Junior League, but that doesn't count because it's not serious stuff. I've talked with her. She hasn't a thought in her head that's her own. She has difficulty speaking to an assembly, so there is no possibility of her taking rhetorical leadership. Watch her, and let me know what you think.

"That's all I have for now, Pierre. Nice chatting with you. I'll leave first."

With that, their luncheon meeting came to an end.

THE NOTE

The next day in the morning, by arrangement, Talent dropped by the home of Elaine Rutherford Blandley, the Board's newest member. The home was the college president's home attached to Bidwell College. They met in her small office located immediately off the front vestibule. Blandley indicated to two student assistants that she would take calls that came in, and that they were to keep her and her guest supplied with coffee and Danish in the library, an adjacent room with bookcases and armchairs.

"Let me start," Talent began, "by thanking you for joining the Board at the Academy."

"I'm glad to do it for you, Bob. It seems like a good cause."

"It is, and you won't have to come to many of the monthly meetings. As for the item I'm bringing with me this morning . . . , I'm afraid it's a little sticky."

"I'm good with sticky things."

"I need a note written," Talent went on, "ostensibly from Petrillo to Langmuir complimenting him on the report he submitted, mentioning how busy he is right now, and encouraging Creston to keep up his good work on the project. The note should serve to keep Creston at work on the project, and deflect him from contacting Tony for a while."

"Let's see what I have here," Blandley responded. "I have a note card with envelope. I use these for casual occasions."

She proceeded to write a kindly note on the card, filling one side of it. She addressed the matching envelope to Langmuir's home. She knew better than to ask about the signature that would be required. She gave the completed card and envelope to Talent. They visited pleasantly for a while before he took his leave.

Talent sat in his car for a few minutes deciding how to proceed. He was twenty miles from his office in the city, and he had an appointment late that morning even farther away. He had to mail it today so that the Post Office would deliver it tomorrow, eight days before the December Board meeting. He took a deep breath and, at the bottom of the note, wrote in script, "Tony Petrillo." As he put the card into its envelope, he was bothered by its appearance. It was obviously an expensive, blue-tinted note-card with a fuzzy edging, and an envelope to match. But there was nothing else to do at this point but take the chance it might backfire. Mail it, and hope that it worked the way it was wanted to work. He sealed it, stamped it, brought it to the local post office, and dropped it in the big blue box.

Note 4: Picking the Fruit

The school headmaster agonizes, "Will this creature ever run out of hidden motives?" Well, no he won't. Takeovers have a secret agenda; so they necessarily are motivated secretly. Only the confederates share this agenda and motivation. That's why I call them a confederacy.

We have, in the visit of the president with the headmaster, and the progress they are making to establish a new kind of academic course, an example of how they set up new policy without the knowledge of the Board. Talent simply misuses the presidential prerogative of confidential meetings with the headmaster. If questioned about these meetings and the new course, however, he can deny policy making: the president was merely helping the headmaster solve an administrative problem in planning a course addition, something that ordinarily does not require the attention of the Board.

Neither the Faculty nor the Board approved the new course. The faculty may assume that it has the approval of the Board, and the headmaster is properly implementing it. The Board may assume the faculty planned the new course as a matter of routine. The faculty will know the new teacher reports, not to the faculty, but to the headmaster, but the Board will be unaware of that.

The prerogative of the president to meet confidentially with the headmaster has important uses that make it a significant relationship. The Board — especially the GC chair — must be on its guard that it not be abused.

5. First Awareness

A NOTE RECEIVED

The note puzzled Langmuir. He hoped Tony might contact him after reading the interim report he had submitted the previous week. "But this?" he thought, "A pretty little note card telling me to keep the project going, but claiming he is too busy to meet right now. Sounds like Tony is overloaded and needs some breathing time."

Langmuir noticed more than that, however. He asked himself, "Does a guy like Tony really distribute flowery epistles of encouragement to his staff and volunteers? And why does he write them on fancy, blue-tint card stock – a dollar each with matching envelope? Female handwriting! One of his secretaries must have penned it for him. Next there was the postmark – from way out of town. Why would the note be mailed from fifteen miles away? I'll have to stay focused on Tony until I have him figured out better."

Langmuir's second Board meeting took place the following week, on a weekday of the first week in December. He studied the names. The only persons he had met were Stoddart, whom he had seen at the Board-staff-faculty reception in September, and Theresa Peterson, who was conversant with the faculty and had a broad knowledge of the Board. He had talked with her at some length; he guessed she was in her early sixties. She was an interesting person, with a smart, business-like demeanor. The published agenda held nothing of interest. There were no policy issues for discussion, nor were there to be reports by committees. It listed eleven items of announcement or presentation.

The evening meeting was held in the cafeteria building of the otherwise closed school buildings. The chairs and round tables were already stacked out of the away except for the chairs they would need, which were arranged in a circle.

Langmuir arrived early and took a seat. He noticed the headmaster and the admissions officer, Mrs. Snow, were there as guests. Quite promptly, another member came over and took the seat beside him, though there were yet mostly empty chairs. The act was so pointed, that Langmuir expected the person would introduce himself and maybe have some matter to bring up. But no, the neighbor looked about as though Langmuir were not there.

"I'm Creston Langmuir," he opened, and offered his hand.

"I'm Pierre de Vanough," his neighbor responded with a handshake. "Welcome to the Board."

Shortly thereafter, the president prevailed upon the members to be seated, and called the meeting to order. He turned his agenda to the matter of school development priorities.

"There has emerged a need to study the school's various activities," he began, "as these each demand resources which are limited. We need to put them into some order of priority. I have asked our Ruth Blanchard to undertake this study as she has experience in matters of this sort. Ruth, would you like to speak to what is planned?"

"How odd," thought Langmuir. "Organizations like this give assignments to committees, not to individuals. In looking over the bylaws this morning to see how extensive they were, I noticed the emphasis they place on committees doing the work of the Board. Group practice, it's called. It's quite the rage in academic circles."

As requested, Ruth spoke up, or tried to, as she had a rather soft voice, "There will be an all-school meeting on some January evening – hopefully one without a snow storm – where we will form study groups. We look for trustees, teachers, and parents to come. We will form small discussion groups for the many activities that are in contention. I will collect from them suggestions and arguments about the desired priorities for our many school activities. Then a report of these findings will be prepared."

"Thank you Ruth," Talent interrupted. "Tony, do you have something to add?"

The headmaster spoke up, "Yes, Bob. We're faced with a lot of academic and non-academic activities to choose from. Each is important. I am familiar with Ruth's background, and on this, she can be expected to do an outstanding job."

The headmaster's endorsement brought a quick end to the topic, and the Board turned quiet for a moment. A member raised his hand to speak. Talent granted the request with a nod.

"The agenda still does not call for reports from the standing committees," said the member in a clear and resonant voice. "I have spoken about this before, and so far with no results."

Langmuir recognized the member as one who was pointed out to him previously. His name is Cator Blackworthy, a representative to the state legisla-

5. First Awareness

ture for the district. The previous president invited him to join the Board as a community outreach measure by the Academy.

Blackworthy continued, "I want to place a resolution on the floor. Is the secretary ready? Be it resolved, that for regular monthly meetings of the Board, the agenda will call for a report to be delivered for each of the standing committees."

Langmuir was sympathetic with the resolution's purpose, but remained quiet.

Another member felt that the passing of resolutions concerning the meeting agenda was a trivial effort. He spoke up, "I don't believe that resolutions ought to be used to try to control the meeting agenda. They should be saved for more substantive matters."

Surprisingly, Blackworthy reacted immediately to this criticism, saying, "I withdraw the resolution."

The president picked up the initiative, and continued his agenda. Routine matters were taken up and disposed of. As Langmuir began to think the meeting might begin to wrap up early, the president opened a subject not on the published agenda. He announced, "Creston Langmuir, for several weeks, has studied the bussing situation at the school. We want to thank him for turning in a thoroughly professional report."

Langmuir's neighbor gently pushed his right elbow off the chair arm causing him to tilt in that direction. De Vanough asked him, in a confidential voice, "Do you think it's better to educate children in private or public schools? I think it's better to educate them in public schools. What do you think?"

"It is perfectly okay to send them here for their education," Langmuir politely responded while trying to listen to the president at the same time.

"But, Creston, is it 'perfectly okay?' Isn't that position necessarily an elitist outlook?"

The president, meantime, continued by introducing the next agenda item for the Board's consideration.

Langmuir now ignored his neighbor's question. He knew at once that the president's words carried a wrong implication, but he couldn't get his mind about it at that moment. Unfortunately, the Board had moved to the next topic. This surprise opening and rapid closing of his bussing topic left him bewildered.

"The president implied," he thought, "that the bussing report he had submitted was the final report and that the project was complete." He was utterly preoccupied over this announcement for the remainder of the meeting. He had never seen anything quite like it before. It would take some careful thinking to decide what to do about it. Fortunately, the meeting was soon over.

A NEW ACQUAINTANCE

To assuage his anxiety, Langmuir got up from his chair and drifted into the kitchen for some coffee and cookies. To his surprise, a voice said, "Creston?"

He turned to see a young, attractive lady of the Board coming over to him from the kitchen door.

"I'm Beth Perwick, Creston. Welcome to the Board."

"Thank you for introducing yourself. I haven't connected the names and faces together yet."

"You're only at your second meeting, and already getting commended for having completed a report on our bussing system. That's pretty good, I'd say."

Langmuir was somewhat taken aback. He decided he did not want to discuss the circumstances of the report now. He would keep things light until he knew what this was about. She certainly was attractive and coming on strong. But he sensed she was married, and decided that would be a safe place to start.

"Thank you, Beth," he replied. "Do you have children in the school?"

"We have two daughters who have graduated from the Academy. The youngest graduated two years ago, and is a junior at state university in the city."

Perwick was pleased to notice they were still alone in the kitchen, so she continued.

"That's why I wanted to speak to you. Someone mentioned to me that you and Sally have a summer place up near Lakeside. Is that right?"

"Yes, we do," Langmuir replied. "Sally's parents lived there for many decades. She spent her summers there as a child. Why do you ask?"

"Well, I hope you don't mind . . . my husband, Steve, is a member of the Lakeside Country Club there, but he doesn't know the young people, only the city members. "Are you and Sally members?"

"Oh yes. The Club is quite a social center. We are active in it in the summertime. And we do know the local people. Is there something we can do for you?"

"I don't mean to impose upon you and Sally, Creston. I hope you understand. But I would like my daughter Alexandra to get some introductions there if that's possible."

Langmuir was amused. He thought, "A mother advancing social opportunities for her daughter. How quaint."

5. First Awareness

"No trouble, Beth. We would be delighted to do so. I'm glad you spoke to me. I was unaware that Steve was a member at The Lakeside Club. I look forward to meeting him."

"Oh, thank you so much," Perwick exhaled. "This place is clearing out. I guess we better get going too. Thank you again."

"Not at all, Beth. Good night."

With that, they headed out into the parking lot and their cars just before the janitor turned off the lights.

A RESIGNATION

Cator Blackworthy went directly home from the Board meeting, arriving about 9:30, and complained to his wife about his dissatisfaction with the meeting. "No one seems to co-operate with anyone else. It's just a collection of individuals paying attention only to what interests it at the moment."

He was getting warmed up on this theme when he was surprised at this late hour by the telephone. He answered it.

"This is Bob Talent," the president said. "You seemed a little miffed by the meeting this evening, especially when you tendered the resolution and it got criticized."

"As a matter of fact," Blackworthy replied, "it did bother me."

"You are not a part of the Academy community are you?"

Blackworthy, surprised by such a comment, said, "No, I'm not."

"And you are not a neighbor of the Academy, are you?"

"No, I live in Chatsworth," Blackworthy answered.

"Do you feel that the Academy Board of Trustees is the right place for you?"

"If you think I'm out of place there, I would offer to resign," he responded.

Talent pushed harder. "Maybe this Academy is not a good fit for you."

"You have my resignation, Bob."

"In that case, Cator, I accept it. You have served the Academy well these several years. You'll remember that we have a reception for present and former members later this month, and you are always welcome to visit the school. I'll confirm this understanding in a letter." With that, Talent ended the call.

Blackworthy explained to his wife that the Academy's Board was the strangest one on which he had ever served.

AN INAPPROPRIATE REQUEST

On his way home after the Board meeting, Langmuir, too, reviewed the meeting carefully.

"De Vanough pushed my elbow immediately when the president finished the second sentence," he remembered. "So, he knew that there would be no more words spoken by the president. Pierre knew exactly what the president would say and when he would finish. He could engage me before I realized the president was done. The two were meticulously coordinated with each other to prevent my speaking up. For a second meeting, it would seem that I have been introduced to the Board rather thoroughly.

"Why did my bussing project come up at a Board meeting? The project originated within the school. It was a school activity. Board members are at least nominally forbidden to put their fingers into school management matters. Is Bob helping to run the school? Even worse, was the bussing project Bob's idea?

"Is the project still active? Clearly not. Obviously, both Tony and Bob consider it finished. But Bob never said it was ended. If challenged, he could deny it.

"The president must have decided to terminate the project together with Petrillo. They never told me of their decision. With Tony's note, they kept me working diligently on the project for another two weeks after they had decided to end it.

"I say 'they,' but Talent must be the driving force. His purpose with me seems to be humiliation. How clever of him! As for Tony, his life under Talent's direction surely is unpleasant.

"So, Talent sets me up with a project; lets me work on it enough to make it my own; then terminates it — bang. But does so without telling me it has been terminated, so I keep working on it. I even get a pretty note of encouragement to make sure I'm working hard on a project that isn't. How very clever of him.

"Am I to take up a fight to finish the project? And, there is the matter of my mortification. How should I respond?

"I have to presume they, or maybe only Talent, want my resignation, otherwise why the extra two weeks of humiliation. Does he perceive me as a threat? A threat to what? He has already achieved the office of president. Does he have plans to stay on for two or four more years? That might make me a threat. What is his ambition?

"Am I expected to call John or Bob and offer my resignation? They, in turn, will accept it with alacrity.

5. First Awareness

"No! My bussing project is dead, I'll leave it at that. But I'll stick around to see some more of this manipulatory artistry."

The next day Langmuir made two phone calls. The first call was to Stoddart, the recently elected chair of the GC, and therefore the Board's purported policeman.

"Hello!" Stoddart was at his desk.

"This is Creston Langmuir. I would like to talk with you about how the Board is presently being managed. Could we meet, please?"

Stoddart replied, "I think that would be inappropriate."

From there the conversation went nowhere; Langmuir closed the call.

He thought, "In his selection of Stoddart, Talent secured his backside."

SOME SNOOPING

Langmuir's second call was to Roger Papalian, the immediate past president. Papalian responded to Langmuir's concerns in a forthright manner. He considered Talent's methods a serious problem and suggested they meet at a coffee shop the following week.

As they settled into a booth, Papalian opened, "Talent sponsored both Pierre de Vanough and Ruth Blanchard for membership before he became president, and he sponsored Blandley's candidacy this fall. None of these three had a connection of their own with the Academy. In my opinion, this gave the president three associates who shared the president's purposes for the Academy, whatever those purposes might be. Their purpose could not be simply that of getting him elected, because that had already been achieved before Blandley came on."

That made sense to Langmuir, who picked up on the theme, "Presumably, a schedule of policy accomplishments is involved. Here we have three confederates who share knowledge of those policy goals. They can be targeted against members who get in the way of those accomplishments as Pierre was targeted against me last week."

"But why you? Have you gotten in the way of anything?"

"No. I've only been around for two months," Langmuir responded. "The next day, I called Stoddart to ask for a meeting, and got nowhere," said Langmuir.

"You won't get anywhere with him," answered Papalian. "Stoddart was selected by Talent as a replacement for Jack Medford. He selected someone who could be made part of the management team, and someone who would only follow instructions. The idea of a Board policeman is repugnant to Stoddart. Pretty smart of Talent, huh?"

"Oh yes, he is smart. How about the committee member Greta Johnson?" asked Langmuir.

"Well, you could try talking to her. But she only joined the Board last June, and she is somewhat sequestered on the committee. She probably cannot undertake, on her own, an action on the GC. That would be quite beyond her capacity, if I have her measured correctly. And, of course, if Talent has her measured correctly."

Langmuir mused aloud, "Protection all around. The GC consists of three: Talent; Greta, a beginner; and John, a follower. Nothing there to pursue. And we suffer an established, functioning confederacy within the Board."

"By the way, Creston, did you know that Blackworthy resigned?"

"No, I didn't. That was sudden."

"I bumped into him at a concert yesterday evening," continued Papalian, "and he said something about how he had a talk with Talent after the Board meeting. The conversation seemed to lead to his offering his resignation without his quite knowing how it came about. Another vote lost. Don't you resign, Creston."

"No, I won't resign. As a matter of fact," explained Langmuir, "in most social organizations like this Board, I usually end up doing my fair share of the president's job. Usually a year or two. I have wondered, Roger, how much of one's time does the job take?"

"I would have a brief phone conversation with Tony about once every two weeks, and that seemed to take care of things pretty well," answered the past president.

With that, and without making definite plans, they parted with the understanding they would stay in touch.

__MORE SNOOPING__

Langmuir's son had entered the Academy in the sixth grade. He was now in the tenth grade, and during these years Langmuir had become friendly with the admissions director, Mrs. Snow. She had, in fact, ever so discretely encouraged the faculty's interest in seeing Langmuir on the Board. The Christmas season gave breathing space to Mrs. Snow, so she welcomed his suggestion that they might have a talk. She suggested her office on a Saturday morning. There they could talk at length without it being noticed, even though her office was opposite that of the headmaster with the office clerical area between them.

5. First Awareness

After much casual talk comparing the Academy with the other private secondary schools in the region, they informally reviewed the progress of Langmuir's son. Then it was school activities past and future. With those things out of the way, they turned to more substantial matters.

Langmuir took the lead, "When my son's affairs have needed some administrative attention, it has been convenient for me to come here on Friday afternoons. On these visits, I have noticed Robert Talent entering or departing the headmaster's office. Does he meet with the headmaster every week?"

The director lowered her voice so it was barely audible, "Yes, every Friday afternoon since the September after he was elected president. The meetings run thirty to sixty or more minutes."

Langmuir realized they were on dangerous turf for Mrs. Snow. He lowered his voice too, "Just the two of them?"

"Yes. Every week the school is in session."

To be certain of what he was learning, he took one more step, "That's an awful lot of time. It's considerably more than Talent spends in his monthly meetings with the Board."

"Yes it is."

Langmuir felt it was a topic too filled with severe implications for Mrs. Snow for him to permit further discussion. The facts alone were quite enough.

They turned to a casual discussion of admissions policy matters for a while. They finished with more friendly talk about families and friends. Afterwards, Langmuir continued to be impressed with the risk Snow was willing to take that he should be informed of a critical matter.

Note 5: Spotting Takeovers

A takeover effort is necessarily secretive. Once a member becomes concerned that something may be wrong, a deliberate effort to learn more becomes appropriate. Fortunately, the most ordinary and wholly acceptable means can accomplish this.

Learn the background of Board members to get ideas of whom to approach about a specific point of interest. Then see if they volunteer to expand on that topic out of their experience and interests. Not surprisingly, such discussions may reveal the most worrisome things happening on the Board.

Board members have documents showing the assignments and the membership of committees. The interested member should collect these documents for several previous years. They will show who has worked with whom and allow one to know whom to ask for various kinds of information. In the example of this chapter, those who served on the previous governance committee, if asked, might identify who were the sponsors of members.

Attend school functions to meet faculty and staff members. If they have reason to be worried about an aspect of the school, some may have the presence of mind and courage to drop a hint of it, even an invitation to meet and talk.

In these ways, learn what is going on, and see if prior concerns get amplified or dismissed. Note how the removal of Board members almost at will is an essential capability for the protagonist. We will see that of the many ways to obtain the resignation of a member, it is surprising how often they leave no witnesses.

Of course, the purpose of an uncancelable term of office for the individual member is to offer the members independent, freely offered, participation. A practice of removing those members who offer a voice corrupts the whole purpose of the Board. To stem attempted resignations, an humiliated member might resolve that not resigning is best. Finally, it will be tempting to openly warn the Board about perceived wrongs. Realize that anyone who does that becomes a troublemaker member and is punished accordingly.

6. The Confederacy

THE GOVERNANCE COMMITTEE

Early spring presented several difficulties for Robert Talent. He had to carefully manage the succession to his presidency for the annual meeting in June. If he were to fail, so that someone of real competence was elected, four years of his efforts would come to naught. So, once again, he called his helpers together at his home.

Talent opened the meeting, "Pierre and Ruth, I would like you to meet Elaine Rutherford Blandley. Her husband is president of Bidwell College. The Board is lucky to have someone of her stature on its Board. Elaine, Pierre de Vanough is president of the Precisional Corporation. Ruth is our lady of leisure, although she keeps busy, very busy indeed, doing good things for the community. I have called you together this evening because there is much to do if the Academy is to be brought along as we want it to be."

Talent began his agenda: "Last fall everything went well, except that Langmuir did not resign as I had hoped."

"What was this about?" asked Blanchard.

"We gave him a project. He got heavily invested in it. Then we pulled it away," explained Talent.

De Vanough asked, "Is he mentally numb and doesn't care how badly he's treated?"

"No. He is just thick-skinned. I think he is something of an intellectual, and won't go away until he has the place figured out. He's proving particularly dangerous. That's where things stand.

"The winter has been quiet. Similarly for the February Board meeting. Except that we took the second vote for the middle school and it easily passed without discussion. While members of the Board had received the headmaster's letter with its planted sentence prior to the meeting, the matter was not raised for comment by a member. We got the middle school approved by the Board as a separate administrative unit. We are done with that ugly duckling.

"Nothing of concern happened at the March Board meeting, as expected; that is why it was not necessary for you to attend it.

"You certainly have quieted the Board," Ruth offered.

"Yes," answered Talent, "it is almost under control."

Ruth continued, "I was at the November meeting, Bob. Talbot made quite an impression with his introductory comments. I don't know whether it was good or bad with his mentioning a charge rate of seven hundred and fifty per day."

"Sorry, I forgot to speak about that. Train made a good impression, Ruth," said Talent. "You don't want the school to become complacent about costs.

"Elaine, Talbot Train has his own consultancy for secondary schools. We have brought him in as a consultant to the Board, but he will be working for me.

"Ruth, your all-school, winter evening went well, but you say you do not want to write the report. Am I right about that?"

"Yes. I have never tried to write something quite that extensive."

"Train is expert at that sort of thing. You put together the material you have collected, any notes you have made, and send them to me."

"That's a relief. It's just not something I think I could do. I'll get my stuff to you. Thank you."

Talent continued, "Train's first task will be to take Ruth's collected material about school priorities and write a full report for the headmaster setting these forth." While affecting a stage smile, he continued, "The finished report will be untouched by human hands, as they sometimes say."

"Elaine," Talent said, as he moved to the next agenda item, "we have tried to get Creston Langmuir to resign, but have not been able to do so yet. That difficulty is one reason we needed your additional help here."

"Is he going to go for president?" she asked.

"Not so far. He is new on the Board. But John Stoddart tells me Langmuir has talked with Roger Papalian, the former president, about that possibility. So, as I say, he's dangerous. He has intrinsic support from the faculty, and that carries weight with the board. Also, he is well spoken, smart, and experienced. So I am very concerned."

Talent moved the discussion to another point. "There is something I want you to be aware of. The faculty, or some members of the faculty, are up in arms against the headmaster.

6. The Confederacy

"Tony does not work well with faculty members. He is afraid of them because of his own lack of academic credentials. His method is to meet with each one alone once a year in his office where, it is said, he sometimes yells at them. The chair of the faculty, Wilson, is a Petrillo loyalist from the history department whose actual job is to shield him from the faculty. I am treating the whole matter as an ugly rumor. Tony is a good boy; he's working with me effectively; I want no changes.

"This evening," Talent began his next item, "we have to start planning for the annual meeting. My term as president will end, but Stoddart's term as Chair of the governance committee will continue for a second year."

"You will not have an office?" asked de Vanough, somewhat alarmed.

"That's right. An attempt to continue would open a pandora's box of discussion in June. Once that started, we would be out of control. I don't know what might happen then. If our exclusive influence on school policy is to continue, we must have a slate made up by the GC that is passed without challenge. There is no other way."

"But you will become an ordinary member."

"That's right," answered Talent, "but I know how to make it work. So we have to find a new president for the Board."

"Bob, how about John, the governance committee chair?" offered Ruth.

"Ruth, we have to leave him alone. Stoddart impresses everyone in his role as an . . . ," Talent again produced the stage smile, "executive-in-waiting. My suggestion," he continued, "is to nominate for president of the Board a graduate of the school for the first time."

"Okay," chided Ruth, "tell us who it is."

"I suggest Beth Perwick."

De Vanough, as requested, had been watching Perwick, "She certainly appears presentable, Bob, but do you really think she can handle the public ceremony that goes with the job?"

"Just barely." Talent addressed the matter, "She went from college right into marriage and raising a family. No work experience. She doesn't know competitive business politics. She is quite innocent. Her husband is a banker in the city. They have two children, the last of whom finished at the Academy two years ago. Most importantly, she cannot address herself easily to an assembly; we will not be risking the possibility of her grabbing rhetorical leadership."

"Can you get the governance committee to go along with this?" asked Ruth.

"Oh, yes. The GC is quite obedient."

He paused to let his helpers get their breath. "I have one more item to be considered," he continued. "Pierre has mentioned repeatedly that Jake Isaac is a real pain in the butt on the Budget Committee. The committee is a combination of Board and school people, so there is little he can do about the problem within the committee. So, he needs to be removed. I will propose Isaac for nomination on the annual slate to the position of Treasurer. And we will take it from there."

No question or comment followed.

Talent wrapped up the meeting, "It's getting late now. We have covered a lot of matters, but, by June, we should be ready for the annual meeting. I meet with the GC next week to advance these items. Thank you all for your continued help. I'll see some of you at the April meeting."

With that, the meeting was over.

THE GOVERNANCE COMMITTEE

The GC, its three members, met in the otherwise vacated school development office after hours on a late March afternoon. Although John Stoddart was the chairman, the meeting was run by Talent. Greta Johnson noticed this and didn't like it; it was the wrong way to do things. She also recognized that three was a difficult number for a committee; there is always the tendency for two to combine their opinions against the third. But she knew it was the Board's most important committee and she took her part seriously.

There were two new candidates for Board membership to be considered. Both were parents, both were well recommended by members and, to some extent, by the faculty. After a short discussion, they were in agreement to present the names to the Board for a vote. With that done, Talent moved them to their principal work of the afternoon, that of building a slate for the annual meeting.

"I have talked with John," Talent offered, to get matters underway. "He has agreed to serve another year as chair of this committee. He plans then to retire from the Board." Looking at Greta, he continued, "If there is no objection, we will place John's name on the slate."

There was no objection.

"I want to bring up something new. From time to time the Board has had a treasurer, but at the present we do not. This summer the school may want to change its banking arrangements. It would be helpful for us to have the office of treasurer available to assist in these changes. Fortunately, we have someone well qualified for such a position — Jake Isaac."

"How long has he been with the Board," asked Stoddart.

6. The Confederacy

"Five years."

"What I have heard of him is that he has been diligent in following the accounting matters that the Board gets into occasionally," continued Stoddart.

"That's right."

Stoddart had more, "Pierre says that his questions on the budget committee are well pointed."

"Indeed, they are."

"Why don't we go ahead, Bob, and put him on the slate for treasurer?"

"Greta, how do you feel about Jake as treasurer?"

"Sounds all right to me," said Johnson.

"Then he goes on the June slate," concluded Talent. "Which brings us to the matter of a president. As you know, I have declined to continue for a second year, simply because there are some on the Board that would object."

"Let me suggest," began Johnson, somewhat timidly, "Wally McCarthy. He's a vice-president over at the Englemark plant. I hear he has fifteen hundred people working under him. Wouldn't he be good?"

Talent spoke up quickly, "People have asked him before, and he says he can't possibly do the job. He is much too busy."

But Johnson had given the nomination of a president some thought, "Rexford Lake has been a member for a considerable time. He's president of the Commercial Realty Corp. in the city. He would make a good president."

"Lake has been around a long time. His company is being investigated right now for involvement in what appear to be some shady deals. It's not in the papers yet, but I expect it will be shortly. We had best avoid him for now," said Talent looking steadily at Johnson.

Johnson was startled. "I suppose so," she said quietly. She thought, "Two quick put-downs in succession. No discussion. John stays silent. This committee is spooky."

Talent got the meeting back on his track, "In thinking over the matter of the next president, what do you think of the idea that it is time for the Board to have for president a graduate of the Academy?"

Stoddart spoke up, "That would be a fine thing to do."

"Greta, what do you think?"

"Yes. That would be good, providing we have someone qualified."

"Let me suggest Beth Perwick. She has been on the Board for three years, with solid attendance. She contributes to the floor discussions at Board meetings. She is personable and intelligent. John, what do you think?"

"Sounds perfectly okay to me, Bob, if you think she can do the job."

"Greta, what do you think?"

"I like her. We have talked a few times, and she seems very friendly."

Talent wrapped it up, "If I don't hear objections, we will put her name on the slate for June. That gives us three names. John, here, for chair of the governance committee, Jake Isaac for treasurer, and Beth Perwick for president. Are we comfortable with that?"

John spoke up, "I am."

"So am I," said Johnson, feeling that there was no place else for her to go.

"In that case, I will speak to Beth and Jake immediately to get their concurrence.

"Otherwise, we're done and the meeting is adjourned. Thank you."

Note 6: Rhetorical Leadership

Rhetorical leadership is the ability to address the assembly with aplomb and precision. A member may use it to expose wrongdoing to the Board. Rhetorical leadership holds a mortal threat to a takeover. The laity will identify careful rhetorical exposition as leadership. A member exhibiting such leadership becomes a candidate for spontaneous nomination to an officer position. He becomes a multiple threat to the confederates.

The matter of presidential succession, which takes place at the annual meeting in June, will necessarily quite consume the protagonist of our story. This is his greatest vulnerability. His election slate must avoid a person who might, once in office, use rhetorical leadership to grab influence away from him.

Also, a member who has the effrontery to spontaneously offer a resolution on the floor for Board consideration and vote, threatens the takeover effort. Attempts of rhetorical argument or of a resolution will mark that member, in the eyes of the confederacy, as a candidate for removal from the Board. Takeover efforts require a silent Board.

Although in many situations this may be difficult to arrange, electing a competent president can be expected to cure a takeover attempt.

7. The Slate

FOR PRESIDENT

The following week, at the end of March, Talent had a brief phone conversation with Train. "Talbot, I just want to confirm that Blanchard's report, setting forth school priorities, is on the headmaster's desk. Did we make it?"

"Yes. I brought it in earlier this week and left it with Claire."

"How nice," commented Talent. "It formally sets forth school priorities for the next several years. And no one got to touch it but the three of us."

"I would think so."

"Very good. Thank you very much, Talbot. I appreciate your help, as does, I am sure, Ruth Blanchard."

"Not at all. Anything else up?"

"Perwick has agreed to stand for president. At the April Board meeting next week," Talent explained, "her nomination for president will be mentioned. We'll see what the reaction is."

"What do you expect?"

"Satisfaction, on the whole. The only legitimate criticism would be that she can't handle the job. Her outlook on events taking place around her is quite limited. She has no idea how to sort people out to make them useful. And there are obviously several on the Board that are more qualified. But everyone will go along with a theme of the first school graduate to become Board president. I expect no one will question it on the floor. We're letting her name out now to preempt those who might want to promote someone else. I don't expect a contention."

"Sounds like you have it under control, Bob. Anything I can do?"

"Not right now Talbot. You are released, so to speak. I don't see a need for you to attend Board meetings this spring. I'll keep you informed of what is happening."

With that, they ended the call.

TUITION POLICY

The meeting was held in the evening at the school. Talent opened it with an announcement, "Welcome to the April meeting of the Board of Trustees. I am pleased to open this meeting with an historic announcement. The governance committee has decided to nominate Beth Perwick for the office of president of the Board. For the school, this is an historic event. Beth will be the first president in the history of the school to be a graduate of it. I am tremendously pleased, and I trust you will be also."

As Talent prepared to move his agenda forward, he glanced at Perwick to see her staring at her desk and blushing profusely. A lady in her mid-forties, of medium height, combed back, shoulder length, beige hair, who loved riding, often appearing in jodhpurs, and sometimes carrying about her a faint odor of the barnyard. She was attractive and otherwise thoroughly presentable. But there remained the question whether she would be able to handle the job even with the heavy amount of attention he planned to give her.

Talent addressed himself to the assembly, "At this time of year, as you know, the Board has the task of approving our tuition rate for the next school year. This rate is the result of considerable effort by the budget committee under Pierre's guidance. That committee, I would remind you, has serving on it key members of the administration as well as Board members. They have had a series of lengthy meetings this past winter where they reviewed the estimated cost structure of the school, the anticipated enrollment, and from that the recommended tuition amount.

"You will notice that there is a considerable jump from last year's rate. Part of that comes about because this year there is an additional element in the tuition. We have considered the need to be able to help those who have difficulty meeting the tuition rates of private schools. To be able to give them more help, the committee has added an additional increment. The Academy will be able to help those who previously could not have considered the school because of its cost.

"You have the numbers in front of you. Are you ready to vote approval of the new tuition rate?"

The former president, Roger Papalian, raised his hand. "Where did this idea of subsidizing some tuition payments come from?"

"From the budget committee, of course."

Two seconds passed without a follow-on question. Talent continued apace, "Are we ready to vote?" A two second pause, "Okay, those in favor please raise your right hand." A plethora of hands went up. "The vote passes. Thank you."

7. The Slate

With the difficult items on his agenda out of the way, the president paused, allowing a quiet to settle across the Board. After a moment Langmuir raised his hand to speak.

"Yes, Creston," the president responded.

"There is something that needs to be mentioned," Langmuir began. "At one time or another, each of us has had the experience, at the end of a meeting, as he is putting on his coat, to glance out the window at the parking lot. There you will sometimes see a gathering of members by a car. . . ."

"Creston," interrupted de Vanough loudly, "there are other people who would also like to have a chance to speak, you know."

Stoddart stared at de Vanough for his uncouth behavior, but said nothing. The president gazed at Langmuir to see how he would take the interruption.

"No one else is asking to speak, Pierre," said Langmuir pointedly. He paused to see if the interruption would grow bigger, but nothing more was said.

He took a moment to get his breath and continued, "What you see happening in the parking lot is a mini-meeting about Board issues where members are expressing their real opinions. Those discussions ought to take place here in the hall, not in the parking lot, nor over the telephone that evening, nor by e-mail over the weekend. Can't we have more discussion of issues at our meetings, and less outside of our meetings? Thank you."

Though he had nicely recovered and finished his homily, he wondered why the confederacy could be so worried about a harmless homily as to expose one of themselves with the interruption.

"Thank you Creston," said Talent.

He moved to the next issue while, in passing, he thought, "There are no committee reports on the agenda, and, even better, no complaint about them, either. How nice."

He offered the last item on the agenda, "Let me announce that Ruth Blanchard's report on school priorities is complete. She turned it in to the headmaster's office last week. Copies of it are available from that office.

"If there is no further business, I declare the meeting adjourned."

As Langmuir left the meeting he thought, "Imagine Pierre bothering to interrupt my little homily. Are they so afraid of rhetorical talk at a Board meeting, that I might be persuasive with the assembly, and capture their attention? Does Talent really feel vulnerable to a little rhetoric?"

The president flagged down de Vanough on his way out and signaled for them to step into an empty classroom to talk. Talent closed the door and they stood by the wall near the door where they could not be seen through the door's window.

"Pierre, we have Isaac on the slate for treasurer. At the next Budget Committee meeting, make sure that the sizable amount of excavation and grading we're planning to do during the summer gets glossed over as a minor, completely routine activity. Don't raise flags about its funding that might attract his attention. Can you manage that?"

"I have already planned the agenda with Goodacre. Jacob will learn nothing about that work or its funding."

"Thanks. You leave first."

A NEW JOB

As it was conventional practice at the Academy for the June transition of officers to be coordinated with the headmaster, after the April Board meeting Talent met with him at their usual conference on the following Friday afternoon. Talent was surprised to notice that they were sitting at a different table — about the same length, but wider.

"How are you Tony? Things seem to be going fine around here, at least as far as I can see."

"Well, I try to keep on top of events, Bob," answered Petrillo. "Today I need to talk with you about our summer plans."

"Exactly," responded Talent. "We have a lot to get done, don't we? Have you decided if there will be time to get the field work done before school starts in September?"

Tony explained, "We have arranged to bring an end in May to the spring athletic schedule ten days earlier than usual. The riding corral and trails survive untouched by this work, so our equestrian summer program can continue as usually scheduled; it will be unaffected by our excavations. I have a firm in tow that can begin the contract work on the very next day after the athletic program ends. He will start excavating the field, preparatory to laying the huge drainage culvert, that very week. That's the first part of the contract work."

Talent advanced the topic, "We have that long gully to be filled in and a re-arrangement and re-grading of the playing fields. Even the tennis courts will be moved. And the dirt has to be re-surfaced or re-seeded to be ready for the fall schedule."

"By September twelfth," finished Tony.

"Can it be done?" asked Talent.

"Yes, it can. And we will do it. The problem is money, that is, cash. We will need to pay the contractor as the work progresses. If there are unforseen difficulties, we have to be ready to authorize extra work, and meet the corresponding payments promptly. The full tag looks like one hundred and five thousand dollars."

Talent offered some thoughts, "Our Second National Bank has been acting pretty fussy about this much credit. On the other hand, a vice-president at the Savings and Loan Bank has shown to me that he would like our business. Maybe that is the place to go. Can you get started into June with enough cash on hand, Tony?"

He responded with assurance, "Oh, yes. We can get into July before we need more funds."

"Okay, let's plan on that. You brief Goodacre, and I'll go over this with de Vanough. He, in turn, will give the budget committee a briefing. Because it is a large committee and we don't want to inadvertently exaggerate the financial risk involved, he will present the project to them as routine summer field fix-up work, and because we will be engaged in competitive bidding for the work, they should keep the whole matter strictly confidential. He will not mention costs; if queried about them, Pierre will explain that there will be a fully detailed review of costs at their first meeting in September."

"I'll do the same. I'll brief my people, and they will soften it," said Petrillo.

Talent moved to the next item. "I spoke with you earlier about the need for a treasurer. The governance committee has selected Jake Isaac for the position. You and your people know him well from budget committee work. If you have no objection, I will offer him the job."

"Jake should do the job well," responded Petrillo. "I would have no concern with that selection."

Talent concluded, "I'll offer him the job, and let you know what he says. But be careful to not include him in our communications until after he is voted in."

Petrillo thought, "Here we go again. He is carefully limiting the man's relationship with his new job. I wonder where Bob is going with this one. I am beginning to feel sorry for Jake already, and he's such a nice guy."

"That's it. Let the weekend begin," said Talent in a jovial manner, and they adjourned.

THE BAIT

Jacob Isaac had served on the Board for three years offering his capabilities as a CPA. He had served on the budget committee for most of that time. Otherwise, his role was inconspicuous. He was much surprised on a Saturday morning in April, when a phone call came from the Board's president.

"Jake, this is Bob Talent. How are you this morning?"

"I'm just fine, I guess, Bob."

"I'm calling, Jake, on behalf of the governance committee. They have been reviewing your work on the budget committee and are very much impressed by it."

"Well, thank you. I'm pleased. I have been working there for some years. Everything seems to be going okay there. At least so far."

"Tell you what's up, Jake. As the Academy grows, and the world of regulations gets more complicated, we have come to realize that the school needs a treasurer. And your name keeps getting mentioned as a possibility. What do you think, Jake? If we offered you the job of treasurer would you accept it?"

"Oh, dear. I don't know, Bob. What's involved in it?"

"Not much more than you are doing, Jake. Maybe a few more meetings. That's about it. The main difference is you would be in on the more important things that are going on. The reason we are asking you is that we need your experience and expertise. What do you say? Can I tell the governance committee that we can put your name on the slate for June?"

"I guess so. I'll try to do my best, Bob."

"I'm sure you will. Thank you very much. I'll pass on the good news to the committee, and I'll keep in touch with you." With that, Talent finished the call.

The slate for June was now ready, or, as we will see, almost ready.

Note 7: The Extended Presidency

Takeover success requires more than getting their man elected president. To significantly change an institute takes more years than the usual office term of the president allows. Either the protagonist serves successive terms, usually a difficult proposition, or his successor is willing to serve under his immediate direction. Either the confederates must serve the successive terms, or malleable members must serve them.

We see in our story how a malleable member is selected for nomination as the presidential successor. Success with this trick depends upon precise evaluation of the candidate. This book does not attempt to teach that particular skill. We are concerned here with how to notice, respond to, and maybe thwart such a nomination procedure.

Furthermore, the criteria for a presidential extender candidate include female (preferably), little experience with the operation of organizations, and only an average level of awareness about social and hierarchical relationships. The misogyny implied with the selection and manipulation of unexceptional females by aggressive males constitutes an important element of what happens in some committees, even as we may abhor it. This particular trait adds another reason to thwart such behavior if possible. Achieving such awareness is the very purpose of this book.

8. Elections

THE CANDIDATE

Talent had phoned Beth Perwick before the April Board meeting to ask if she would accept the job. When she did, he asked if it would be all right by her to mention it at the meeting. He wanted to see the response.

Fortunately, no question was raised of her suitability. Also, he watched carefully during the May Board meeting to see if concerns had developed, if there was a whispering of concerns, or if something was brought up on the floor, but nothing developed about her then either. It appeared that no one would seriously question Talent's selection — except, as we will see later, Talent himself.

Perwick was excited by the idea of being president of the Board; most people would assume she was president of the Academy.

The next week, at Talent's request, John Stoddart called a meeting of his committee in his home — a deliberately casual setting — on a Thursday evening. Its purpose was to put forward the new president-designee, Beth Perwick, on her first activity — to a small group. She was nervous, even feeling a little jittery, at the thought of her first exposure.

"Will the committee ask me questions about the school's future?" she thought. "God, I hope not. I don't know what I'd say. I hope this meeting will be some kind of love-in. The committee wants to do the election slate for June. That's a good topic for my first meeting, except Creston's name needs to go on it, too.

"He's good," Perwick continued her thoughts. "Wrote a nice letter to me about doing a vice-president stint and having a new committee on academics. I don't know what such a committee might do, but it can't do any harm. The faculty would love it. And there is the matter that he and Sally have a posh place up in Lodan County where my Alexandra, and maybe her sister as well, needs to get some introductions at the Lakeside Country Club. As long-time summer residents there, Creston and Sally can do that. He'll appreciate this V.P. position a whole lot."

Betsy Stoddart answered the door. "This must be Beth. I'm Betsy Stoddart. It's a pleasure to meet you. Come in. The others are already here — in the living room. You know them, I'm sure."

The hostess led Perwick into the living room, where the others were enjoying some nourishment.

Perwick mused, "How could it be that everyone else seems settled in? I know I'm early. Did the meeting really begin earlier than I was told?"

"Can I get you coffee or tea?" asked Betsy Stoddart. She addressed herself to the group, "Then I disappear. I insist upon being banished from my own living room. You can have your little meeting just as you please."

Waiting in the living room were Robert Talent, Greta Johnson, and John Stoddart. Perwick nervously nodded "hello" to each of them and took a seat. Looking around, she thought, "They look friendly enough. I hope this meeting turns out to be mostly a social affair."

"Welcome Beth to the governance committee," Talent began. "Preparations for the annual meeting are complete. So we want to bring you up to date on our plans."

Talent ran through a number of items of current activity, "With regard to the annual meeting, John will be continuing in his current capacity as chair of the GC."

Perwick could only wonder, "Why isn't John conducting his own meeting?"

"There has been one addition since I last spoke to you," Talent continued, looking at Perwick. "Jake Isaac will be on the slate for treasurer. He has done good service for the Board. We thought we would reward him with the title. Other than that, everything is just as I told you."

Talent thought, "Now for her. We'll see how well she does."

He spoke directly to her, "You seemed to be comfortable, Beth, with the extra attention you got at the April and May Board meetings."

"Oh," responded Perwick, "that was nothing. No, I'm perfectly comfortable." She thought, "I probably should have more to say than that. But I don't know what. Maybe this is the time to take care of my one item."

"One thing I want to do," she continued, "is add to the slate Creston Langmuir for vice-president."

The response was silence. As the seconds ticked by Perwick wondered, "Why doesn't anyone speak? Why is no one offering assurance that his name would do just fine on the slate? What is wrong with what I said?"

Talent broke the silence, "I know you are new at this, Beth, but candidates for the slate are usually discussed by the committee and voted upon."

"Not always, Bob," said Johnson. "We haven't voted upon the names so far. Isn't that right, John?"

"Well, I don't know about that," answered Stoddart.

"If that's the procedure," said Perwick, "let's get on with the discussion and voting. Langmuir is a strong member of the Board. And Bob, he did a report for the school last fall that you admired. The faculty is in a very disturbed mood right now, and Langmuir is in touch with them. I need him as a vice-president."

"Oh dear," thought Johnson, "this is trouble. Bob isn't going to like this."

Again, Talent had to break the silence. "I cannot see him as an officer of the Board. I don't think he's reliable. He has not been a committee chairman. I am against putting him on the slate."

Perwick considered to herself, "Vice-presidents come free; you can have as many of them as you want. Langmuir is a perfectly nice guy; there is nothing wrong with him. Isaac has not been a committee chair either, but he is put on the slate for treasurer simply because he has been a good guy. And Greta says the others have not actually been voted on. What's wrong with me? Why can't my recommendation go? Is this what it means to be a female on this Board?"

Perwick spoke up, "I see no reason why Langmuir's name can't go on it. I think he would be good as vice-president about academics. So, I ask you to put him on it."

Talent was in a panic. "Have I blundered?" he thought. "She is way out of control and we have hardly begun. I've got to have a talk with this woman. For starters, let's get out of this place before a vote comes up."

He spoke up, "We have not had a chance to think about this idea. I don't think we are going to get anywhere with it tonight. I suggest we close the meeting."

Perwick was crushed. She wondered, "This can't be. What is happening? Why doesn't John say anything? What is wrong with me? Why can't they accept me?"

A few pleasantries were managed among them as they worked their way out of the Stoddart house and into their separate cars.

<u>ADJUSTMENTS</u>

Talent called Perwick a little too early the next morning. For hours he had blown hot and cold on what to do about Perwick's sudden sponsoring of Langmuir. He regretted his outspoken objection to Perwick's request. He argued with himself,

"I have thought to invite Perwick to a one-on-one with me to change her mind about Langmuir. But on consideration, I don't dare try that now. Time doesn't allow me to maneuver her attitude roundabout before the annual Board meeting. It would be too dangerous as she clearly has her own head going, and the meeting is next Wednesday. I will have to take care of Langmuir afterwards, unfortunately, while not having the advantage of working as an officer."

Perwick answered, "Good morning, Bob."

"Good morning, Beth," said Talent, in that moment regretting the invention of caller-identification. "As you may guess, I'm calling about the meeting last evening. The Langmuir matter needs resolving one way or another. At this point, though, I'm willing to go along with putting his name on the slate."

Perwick wondered, "Did Bob talk with John and find that he supported Langmuir? If so, it might have been two against one if a vote were taken." She responded, "Will you call a second meeting of the committee to take a vote on it?"

"We don't need to bother with that. Langmuir's name will be down as vice-president on the slate."

"Will you call John and Greta to let them know?"

"No need to. They will be at the meeting. There won't be things happening they don't know about."

Perwick wondered to herself, "So that's how the committee works. Talent just runs it as he pleases. I can't understand why John isn't interested in doing his part. Seems I did all right last evening. I stood by my request about Langmuir, and it went my way. Good for you, girl."

Talent moved on, "You know that the school will be doing extensive excavating this summer to lay a new drainage conduit under the soccer fields. The layout of the several fields and the tennis courts need to be rearranged to make use of the new area provided by the drainage improvement."

"Oh yes. I have followed that. I see work has begun."

"Well, the work has to be done on a tight schedule to be ready by the start of school in September. The contractor has to be paid installments during that time. I plan to continue to work with the building and grounds committee, the treasurer, and the headmaster during the summer to make sure all goes well."

Perwick responded with a voice of authority, "Please do. I appreciate your help, Bob. That work is critical. And keep me informed."

"I'll see you next Wednesday at the meeting," Talent said, and closed the call.

ELECTION

The annual meeting of the Board presented itself quite awkwardly for Talent. The bylaws provide that an elected officer assumes his new post immediately. There is no grace period. Since one cannot be sure who will win the election, the meeting with its agenda must be planned by the current president. To carry out the agenda, elections should get the last place. But that invites jeopardy; it gives people too much time to think. If they are to be well led, it is better to have them vote quickly. He decided, in this, to hedge the bylaws, a not uncommon practice of the Board.

Fortunately, members seemed to show up early that evening, and Talent could call the meeting to order a bit ahead of time. "Would members please take their seats," he hollered to get them in out of the hallways. "Welcome everyone. It is a lovely, early summer evening, and I appreciate your giving it up for this important meeting."

"If the secretary," he began, "will take the attendance and let me know if there is a quorum present."

"There is Mr. President."

"We have a number of things to get done tonight," he said, "including the election of officers. I suggest we turn to that first. John Stoddart's governance committee has prepared a slate of nominees as follows: Beth Perwick for president, John Stoddart for GC chair, Jacob Isaac for treasurer, and Creston Langmuir for vice-president."

Talent cringed a little as he thought, "Now comes the scarey part of managing this gang. The part that is necessarily uncontrollable. There are at least three members whose employment rank alone qualifies them to be president of this place. If one of them were to be elected president, it is most likely my infringement of presidential prerogatives would no longer be tolerated. My plans would come to naught."

He spoke up, "The floor is open to nominations."

Talent counted the seconds. No one raised their hand. After seven seconds, he announced, "Nominations are closed. May I have a motion for the secretary to cast a vote for each of the candidates to be elected by unanimous vote?"

"So moved!"

"Those in favor," continued Talent, "please vote 'aye' by raising your hand." After a pause, "Those opposed. The election slate is carried".

He relaxed, "How nicely it went. We are ready for another year. Perwick is showing no interest in taking over the gavel. So," he thought, "I'll continue on my course."

An engraved captain's chair was awarded to a parting member of long standing. Several other members who were departing were given kind but brief eulogies and an engraved aluminum tray for their several years of service to the Academy. Talent reminded them of the date for the headmaster's reception for Board, faculty, and staff in late September prior to their first Board meeting in early October. He wished everyone a pleasant summer. With the meeting agenda complete, Talent offered the gavel to Perwick, who accepted it.

"Thank you, Bob," Perwick began, "for your service to the Academy as president. I know from working with you that you have been diligent and successful in your duties. Thank you again.

"I also," Perwick continued, reading from notes, "want to thank the Board for its vote of confidence in me, and I will do my best to deserve it."

Then, she moved the Board to a difficult matter. "As you may have heard, some members of the faculty are bothered by a number of things that have happened lately. I want us to give some attention to it. Therefore, I'm calling a special meeting of the Board for the second week in July. You will be notified by e-mail of the time and place. I ask that you do your best to make the meeting because of its importance."

This amazed Talent. Just calling a meeting of the Board like that without mentioning it to anyone beforehand put him back in panic mode. "I've got to have a talk with that woman," said Talent to himself for the second time. "She is running away with the place."

Shortly after that, the Board's annual meeting was adjourned.

Note 8: A Disabled GC

We see in this chapter the importance of disabling the governance committee. Four long-time members on the GC with informed opinions about candidates would open discussion and they would not dodge committee voting. The committee, not the president, would determine the outcome.

Placing a new Board member on the GC is an ingenious twist. Few members of the Board will appreciate that a new member is unable to participate meaningfully in the deliberations of the committee. Nor will the members note that the appointee's year is, for her, wasted time. The appointment is window dressing for the Board.

The chair of the committee plays a critical part. Placing a confederate there would be risky, but that would do the job. We have seen with John Stoddart, as with the successor president, that the selection and election of someone thoroughly presentable but utterly without imagination and initiative can work well for the protagonist.

9. That Woman

PRESIDENT PERWICK

Beth Perwick felt good about herself and her new job as president. She knew she was a particularly attractive woman to whom the added recognition she now received served to ease her initial anxieties. Outside of her family, she had never been responsible for affairs that involved other people. Here, at the Academy, there were not only the other Board members, but faculty, students, staff, and their budgets.

She gave these matters a shot at serious thought, "Where do I start? Who do I turn to? Will they get angry with me if I don't know what to do? The faculty is already upset. But with Tony, not me. Some say he doesn't speak to classroom matters and hides behind Wilson, while others say he is okay. Who do you believe?

"My first meeting with Tony went nowhere, which worries me. He passed over the subjects I brought up in an offhand way that annoyed me. I wanted to go back to them, but couldn't figure out how. I said he was not invited to the July meeting of the Board because we were going to talk about the faculty concerns. He dismissed them as rumors. Wilson, he said, had looked into them carefully and found that they were merely personal gripes of one sort or another. That's what he said. Who do I believe?

"Maybe I should ask Langmuir about this. It was great getting him elected. I insisted and I won. I can do it!

"I have to be ready for the special July Board meeting. We will talk about the faculty problem and I will suggest having Creston look into it for the Board. Maybe do some interviews to find out more about the complaints."

Although it was held in the middle of July, the Board turnout was almost complete. President Perwick brought the meeting to order.

"I know some of you have had to adjust your summer schedules to be here tonight," she began. "I thank you for that. The formal organization of the Board with its committee structure will happen at our first meeting in the fall.

"The topic for this meeting concerns faculty complaints we have heard about for the past several months. We should not talk about them now, repeating what we have heard. That would be repeating rumors. Mostly, they complain the headmaster does not listen to the teachers. Is there any discussion about this?"

Talent watched her thoughtfully. He wondered, "What is she trying to accomplish here with these members gawking at her? Nothing will come of it, I expect. I hope she doesn't get into trouble with it before we have a chance to talk."

As Talent expected, the Board was silent. But, after a considerable pause, a member raised his hand.

"We don't know, really, who is complaining about what, do we? We have to find out what is being said and whether it is true."

Perwick liked that suggestion. She picked up on it.

"I would like to appoint two members to do interviews together," said Perwick. "Would that do?"

The same voice spoke up, "Yes, that's what we should do. By September we will know where we stand with the faculty."

"Could I have a motion to do that?"

"So moved."

Perwick was in full swing. "Are we ready to vote on having two members interview teachers to find out what is wrong?"

Silence.

"Those in favor?"

Many hands went up, but not the hands of Talent or de Vanough or Blanchard or Blandley. The motion passed.

Perwick continued, "Thank you very much. I appoint Creston Langmuir and Theresa Peterson to do the interviewing." Addressing herself to them directly, "We will get together shortly to plan how the interviewing will be done."

Talent re-resumed his previous two instances of panic, thinking, "She is going to run away with this. She's promoting Langmuir to a prominence on the Board from which he will ruin my work. I've got to speak to that woman right away."

Again, Perwick thanked them for breaking into their summer activities to get this decision made and underway. She reminded them of the coming reception in late September for faculty, staff, and Board, and, the following week,

9. That Woman

the October Board meeting. There was some further small talk, and Perwick dismissed her first Board meeting.

"Again, I did it," thought Perwick as she left the school that evening. "I held a meeting, and got done what I wanted to do. Next week I'll meet with Creston and Theresa to make up a list of those to be interviewed. I'm going to like this job."

THE END OF INNOCENCE

A couple of days later, Talent phoned Perwick to set a date for them to meet. They both were busy with the usual family obligations and travel of summertime. The earliest they could meet was in mid-August, for which they chose a nearby country club where Perwick had membership where she used their tennis courts. The club had a small conference room just off the lobby, furnished with comfortable armchairs, a coffee table, and two windowed doors, that was available to be reserved by members.

Perwick had kept in mind Talent's objection to Langmuir. She knew instinctively that it would be a long and, likely, a difficult meeting. She arranged coffee service for two for a ten o'clock, meeting.

There was a slight embarrassment on her part about the hefty tote-bag she carried with her containing much of her trustee file papers collection. One could never know which piece of paper, which documents, might be needed at the moment. She was aware that others did not carry about such a load, especially Talent. He never seemed to be carrying about with him a single paper item. Such differences puzzled her.

She arrived early to be sure the arrangements were in place.

"Good morning, Beth," announced Talent, coming across the lobby. "Isn't it a glorious summer morning?"

"It sure is, Bob. Too bad we have business to do."

"Well then, let's get it over with."

Perwick led the way into the room with its service in place. Talent shut the door and opened the discussion.

"How are you coming with organization of the Board?"

Perwick was dismayed at the question. She remembered an increasing tendency of hers to worry about that particular topic during the ten weeks since the election. She realized that she didn't know exactly what it was about the Board that needed to be reorganized. A copy of last year's committee structure was in her bag, but she resisted the impulse to dig for it. She remembered a question that kept coming to mind. Maybe this was an opportunity to ask it.

"I'd like to ask a question about that," Perwick ventured.

"Certainly."

"How do you select those who should be committee chairs?" she asked, all the while thinking, "I hope he doesn't laugh."

"The committee chairs you already have will do fine for the coming year. Are there some that you have doubts about?"

Perwick thought, "That answer doesn't help except for me to keep the ones he put in place. I guess he doesn't plan to be very helpful." She answered, "No, I have no objections to them. Probably, member assignments to the committees were okay, too?"

Perwick did not quite recognize that she was asking a question.

"There is only one addition I would recommend," answered Talent. "Janet Withers is a most capable member. I recommend adding her to Peterson's committee which is understaffed."

"Sure, we can do that," said Perwick, thinking, "Why her, there? Placing people is a mystery to me." She went to her next subject, "I am thinking of two additional committees for this year."

"What are they?"

"An academic committee and a professional committee. The first comes with Langmuir. That is what he will do. He suggested the other, a professional committee."

Talent responded strongly, "Giving him two committees is wrong. No one else has two committees. Beth, that is wrong policy."

Perwick also responded strongly, "No. He would have only the academic committee. I am thinking of Donna McCarthy. She served on a committee with me. I've gotten to know her."

"What is the professional committee to do?"

"Creston says that the school needs to upgrade its review and acceptance policy for new teachers. He suspects that once they are hired they become permanent, without adequate review after a probationary period."

"Does the faculty agree with that?" challenged Talent.

"I don't know," answered Perwick. But she was thinking, "Maybe I've gotten in too deep on this one."

"I suspect, Beth, that your Creston is way off base on that one," he responded, guessing that she could not deal with the subject. "You go ahead with the committee, but don't let it meet until we have talked about it further."

9. That Woman

Perwick didn't respond. The phrase "your Creston" reverberated in her head, obliterating all else. She had lost track of their relative positions. She managed to pull her thoughts together sufficiently to mention one last concern about the Board's organization.

"Shouldn't we add a few members to the governance committee? After all there has been only one member appointed to it. That is not very many."

Talent worried about this one, but he was in a strong position. He decided to be aggressive. "Let me explain to you how that committee works, Beth. If a member wants to cause you trouble, he runs to the GC and looks there for a sympathetic appointee. Stoddart knows better than to respond to such tactics, but an appointee might take such things seriously. Do you realize the trouble they can cause you? You are advised to leave the GC just as it is for your own good."

Perwick realized he was speaking down to her. It left her feeling a little shaken up. She thought, "What can I do but drop the subject?"

Talent now considered the meeting to be his. After a decent pause to let the atmosphere cool a bit, Talent moved to his agenda. "I want to bring you up to date, as I promised, about the athletic-field landscaping work underway. As you know, the fields must be ready to play on by the third week of September. The contractor seems to be on schedule. As best I can tell, everything will come out as it should."

"That sounds very good."

"It has not been easy. The contractor requires monthly payments. We have had to borrow one hundred and five thousand dollars pending receipt of tuition money in the fall. Last spring, when these arrangements were being set up, Tony and I decided to change banks during the summer vacation time. So, we have a new bank," Talent concluded.

"Well, I'm glad everything is going good."

He promptly moved to the next agenda item, one that was more difficult.

He opened gently, "Could we talk about your plan to interview faculty members?"

"Yes, of course."

He moved assertively to what he planned to make of this meeting, "Do you realize that what you will collect is so much hearsay? What good is hearsay? What can you do with it? And you have committed the whole Board to it. I find it most embarrassing."

Perwick was unnerved. Talent noticed that she flushed from her neck to her forehead.

"Damn him," thought Perwick. "Why can't we just discuss things? But I have to say something." She went ahead, "Bob, we will do what we can with it. That's better than staying ignorant of what concerns the faculty."

In a lowered, even, and soft voice Talent ended the matter, "We can talk another time about what to do with the collected remarks of the faculty. Meanwhile, be sure to keep them under wraps. Don't distribute them, or have meetings about them."

After a pause, Talent continued in a voice that was pure reasonableness, "A more appropriate course for us to take, Beth, would be to meet with Tony and someone from the faculty to see what can be resolved. It's simply a more direct path for us to accomplish something."

"I'm willing to try that."

"Set up a meeting for some time in the next four weeks for us in Tony Petrillo's office, and bring in someone who can represent the faculty. Tony will know who to ask."

"Okay," said Perwick.

But she was in a swivet. She thought, "This is awful. He's co-managing with me. And I can't stop him. There's this matter of Tony's office. Will Bob keep up his weekly, one-on-one meetings with him after the start of school? That's supposed to be my prerogative. If he does, what can I do about it?"

Perwick was miserable. Talent had undone her first initiative, and he was now her co-president.

TURNING PERWICK'S HEAD

"Now Beth," Talent pressed on, "There's a sensitive matter that must be discussed between us."

Beth cringed, thinking, "How many topics does he have? Why does he have to push me on so many things at once? I can do okay by myself, if he would just let me."

Almost rudely, she let out an audible sigh.

"I know this is difficult, Beth," Talent condescended, "but you have not had much opportunity to experience management problems, and here we have a serious one. My concern is with Creston Langmuir, and especially with his position as a vice-president."

"The faculty likes him. I want him to work on academic stuff. What's wrong with that?"

"Nothing at all. He can do those things. But there are other considerations."

9. That Woman

Perwick remained quiet.

Talent brought up the difficulty, "Langmuir has habits that are dangerous to the school, Beth. As president, you have to be aware of things like that and deal with them appropriately or you'll get the academy in great trouble."

"What are you talking about?"

"Langmuir makes snap decisions. He just does something suddenly, without careful consideration. When you are an officer of an academy, a habit like that puts the whole school in danger."

"How do you know that?"

Talent was riding high. He continued, "I watched him work on the bussing project. He was asked to do a study. Instead he started driving the busses about. On an impulse, he drove one to a body shop and asked the cost of making changes. He kept on in that self-centered way without ever going over things with Tony. And especially, without going over things with Tony first, before rushing out and doing them. That kind of behavior is bad enough for someone on the Board, but in an officer it can be harmful to the place."

Perwick was defeated again. "I didn't know about that."

Talent gently said, "I know you didn't. I hope in the future you will ask first, before you commit yourself to some action you may later regret."

She quickly pulled herself together. She ventured, "Where he is concerned with academic matters and working with a committee, he should not be any trouble to us."

Talent loved the "us." She was coming along just fine. He immediately moved the discussion up to the next level. "Not quite, Beth. I have two witnesses who say that he is moving to become president of the Board."

"He is?"

"Yes. Last fall he met with Board member Rexford Lake, the son, at his office downtown to talk with him about his interest in gaining the presidency. Afterward, Rexford junior passed on that word to his father who, as you know, is also a member. If you ask them, they will both tell you that Langmuir has his eye on becoming president."

"What can we do about it?"

With, "we," Talent had reached home base. He answered, "You will have to play a strong role in constraining him. Keeping him from doing anything outrageous. You will have to watch him closely. I want you to attend the meetings of his committee and listen closely to everything he says."

"Okay, I can do that."

"Keep in close touch with me should he suddenly go off on a tangent. I'll let you know what steps to take."

There were two items of constraint for which Talent did not dare wait.

"You will have to tell Creston fairly soon that you will not accompany him when he visits Tony to talk about his academic topics. Otherwise you become a participant in his mistakes."

"Okay. I'll talk to him before the first Board meeting."

"And finally, Beth, at the meeting, I don't want you to announce the formation of Langmuir's committee. That, too, involves you in his doings. Ask him to announce it himself."

"Okay."

Talent moved to his coup d'état. "What we have agreed to, Beth, means that you must avoid meetings of the officers of the Board. Such a meeting will encourage and enable Langmuir into heaven knows what. So, no officer meetings for the present."

Perwick let out a breathy, "Alright."

Perwick had suffered yet another defeat, but what was she to do in the circumstances? Quickly after that, they ended their meeting and Perwick retired to the tennis courts.

Note 9: Subordination

We have seen previously the subordination of the headmaster of the school, and now the subordination of the successor president of the Board. She loses the high-horse that naturally comes with her new title.

Our protagonist points out to her that she, in her first act, was moving the school into a position of danger to its long continuance. To advance his purposes further, he assumes a condescending stance toward her: "As president, you have to be aware of things like that and deal with them appropriately or you'll get the academy in great trouble." She accepts that she is culpable and humbles herself: "I didn't know about that."

Talent has to be sure that she will protect him from the appointment of activist members to the GC. He does this by pretending the danger is to her: "Do you realize the trouble they can cause you? You are advised to leave the GC just as it is for your own good."

The final danger to our protagonist from a new president derives from meetings of the officers of the Board. Perwick meeting with Stoddart and Langmuir poses multiple dangers. Langmuir could easily take rhetorical leadership there, and start educating the other two about those sudden resignations, not to mention identifying the members of the confederacy for them if he has figured them out yet. Talent directs her, "So, no officer meetings for the present." This denial leaves Perwick with no place to turn for advice or even sympathy, except to Talent; she, too, is isolated. Beth Perwick becomes dependent upon Talent for guidance, and with that, these understandings assume a permanent place during her tenure.

Talent leaves Stoddart in his job, and takes on the risk of not being an officer for a year. He always keeps as low a profile as possible. His confederates do also with only de Vanough chairing the budget committee. He does not want anyone to socially map the Board and learn of his and his confederates' actual roles.

10. Harness Fitting

THE DIMINISHED ROLE

They met in the headmaster's office in early September. Talent, Perwick, and Petrillo joined by chairman of faculty Wilson and the Math Dept. chair Dorothy Huang, for the faculty. No introductions were necessary. Each behaved cautiously as they were well aware they had an explosive though elusive topic at hand.

As the host, Petrillo should have opened the meeting. But he, unfortunately, was the subject; he was in the dock. Alternatively, Perwick might have opened it. But she was uncertain of her position, and did not have words ready.

Therefore, as usual, Talent, arguably the lowest ranking person in the room, opened the meeting.

"We are faced with serious rumors to the effect that some faculty members are unhappy, Tony, with your management of the school. My own feeling concerns the potential damage that such talk offers to the Academy. Unfortunately, the Board has initiated a program to interview members of the faculty, which activity will tend to legitimize these rumors. I hope that this morning we can move ahead of that activity."

Perwick fumed. She thought, "So we are being told that my efforts to respond to the faculty complaints are doing damage to the school."

Petrillo responded, "I agree with you, Bob, but I'm the first to admit that I have some rough edges. I would be glad to meet with members of the faculty to discuss their complaints and see what can be done so as to get everyone in this boat pulling on their oars together."

Wilson backed him up, "The faculty is a very diverse group, for which we are much blessed. In any large group there are bound to be those who see things disadvantageously, and we have an obligation to respond to them, just as long as we do not disadvantage the whole academy."

This fine-reasoned talk distracted Perwick. She was reacting with some alarm over the status of her rôle as president. She wondered, "Did these four meet earlier, decide on a course of action, and rehearse their parts before this meeting?"

She spoke up, "We have to let those who have a complaint have their say. I don't think there is danger to the Academy in doing that. We will have to have meetings with those who have complaints."

Dorothy Huang took her turn, "It is important to recognize that there may be some corresponding danger to the Academy in not listening to faculty concerns. I personally see no danger in hearing out those who have complaints. This meeting, this morning, is not, I believe, the proper forum for their complaints to be aired. But a seminar-like session to hear them can be arranged."

Talent worried what that kind of an approach might lead to. He had an almost ideal relationship with Tony for his purposes, and didn't want to risk it by allowing a procedure that had a chance to blow up, as did the course being taken by Perwick.

He decided to take issue with those suggestions. "The school year has just started this week. It behooves us to help it get off with a strong start. I would not want us to consider steps that might roil things that need attention at this start of the new school year." Talent continued, "The Board, as you know, will be interviewing those faculty members who have concerns. They will also interview Tony, so he can have his input. These interviews will take place with one person at a time. The interviewers will offer a report. I suggest that we look at that report to see what is revealed, and take things from there."

Perwick wondered, "What happened to the 'hearsay' problem. Seems it's only a concern when I do it. When Bob needs the interviews, they are okay."

Tony spoke up. "What do you think of Bob's suggestion?" he said, looking at Wilson.

Wilson knew his duty, "That seems to be a good compromise. The faculty should be willing to go along with it. Don't you think so, Dorothy?"

Huang was not in a position to argue further. She acquiesced, but with some strength, "I will be very interested to see what the interview report has to offer."

Talent moved to adjourn the meeting before new doubts arose, "I want to thank each of you for your generous attitude toward this difficult matter. Tony and Beth will stay on this topic and keep in touch with you. Now, let's get the school year running."

Petrillo finished the meeting, "I assure you I will stay on this matter. I will keep in touch with you. And, as Bob has said, let's get this year underway."

10. Harness Fitting

Everyone got up to leave. Only Huang was left wondering about the part being played by Talent. She thought, "Isn't Perwick to be allowed her presidency?"

HARNESS SORES

In her home that evening, Perwick was thinking the same thing.

"Since early September," she thought, "Talent has called me each day with something to discuss. Almost seven times a week. The days I take note of are those when he doesn't call. I must ask him to stop, but what if he continues? What can I do?

"I've agreed to haul-in Creston, as he asked. I agreed to bypass faculty interviewing with the meeting in Tony's office. But he keeps on calling, and pushing.

"Worse than that, Bob meets each Friday afternoon with Tony in his office. That didn't stop when I became president. I wonder what they talk about. As members of the Board, we are not allowed to get involved in school management. The Board hasn't produced policy items to be discussed with the headmaster, but that would fall on me, not Bob. They sure worked smoothly together at the meeting this morning.

"I created the Langmuir problem and I have to do something about it. I'll see what the interviews come up with. Langmuir and Peterson should report their results to the Board at our October meeting. But where do I go with it from there?"

The phone rang. It was Talent.

"I thought the meeting went well, Beth."

"Yes it did, Bob."

"I have a thought for the interview report. When will the interviews be done?"

"Creston and Theresa are to report at the October Board meeting in three weeks."

"What I'm thinking, Beth, is why not have them report to the professional committee? We plan to leave that committee fallow for a while, don't we? So it's available, and the title of the committee is most appropriate."

Perwick was surprised at the suggestion, "But the Board will be expecting their report. It was the Board that asked them to do it."

"No problem, Beth. I will ask Talbot to attend the professional committee meeting. You introduce him as a consultant helping us with the faculty problem. He will then give the Board a report that moves the Board away from your two interviewers, to the action in Tony's office. He will give to the Board a summary of the report, plus what was accomplished in Tony's office. That should keep them happy."

"That sounds all right. I'll tell Creston when I see him at the school reception next week that he will be reporting to the professional committee."

"Good. You'll have to fill out the committee with appointments for the occasion, but, Beth, be careful not to put members on it that ask questions."

With that advice, Talent closed the call.

"How the hell do I know who will or won't ask questions?" thought Perwick. "Is it fair to have Creston and Theresa report to a pseudo committee instead of the Board? They'll probably realize it afterwards and be angry at me, and they are both awfully nice people. But I caused the 'your Creston' problem, so I have to do something about it. I'll see him at the reception."

Perwick was now quite unhappy with her presidency.

Note 10: Harness Fitting

Talent is confident that he has Perwick in tow. He has been sufficiently severe with her that, so far, she cannot bring herself to challenge him again. Perwick's caution arose because she doesn't want to get hurt again.

Talent's machinations bewilder Perwick: "What happened to the 'hearsay' problem? Seems it's only a concern when I do it. When Bob wants the interviews, they are okay." But she is not clever enough to unravel them.

Talent, besides bracing Perwick, is anxious to move decisions about the faculty problem away from the assembled Board and into his (shared with her) control. A select few will make policy for the Academy, even if that few counts up to only one.

Let's take a moment to chart the confederates' outlook. In the story, the confederates have meetings where they openly display their attitude: How they see and justify to themselves what they are doing and the means they are using. This attitude, that the management of the Board and the manipulation of its members may ignore custom, decency, the bylaws, and the law, begs explanation:

They do not see manipulative assaults upon members of the Board as wrongs, nor do they see their actions as harmful to the governance of the Academy. They do not see the disabling of the governance committee as harmful; the placing of unqualified Greta Johnson on the GC as wasteful; the interfering with a speaker as depriving the Board of member comments; the ending of collegiality as harming the members, the Board, and the Academy. These things and more are done determinedly and skillfully to advance their cause, that of having Robert Talent unilaterally modify the operation, staffing, and teaching within the school.

From their point of view, they would concede that they are working a little outside the accepted box. True, they occasionally behave roughly, but their cause more than justifies their methods. It is unfortunate and inconvenient that they must work furtively, a circumstance that arises from the more limited perspective of other Board members. Except for that one circumstance, their work could be done openly.

They are quite unaware of the exceptional degree to which they diverge from accepted norms of behavior. Wasting the time, treasure, and commitment of other members is not a consideration, and a concern for comity among members would be for them tantamount to quitting.

11. A Third Resignee

LANGMUIR BOUND UP

Anthony Petrillo was in fine form hosting his Board-faculty-staff reception in the school cafeteria one evening in late September. He was a naturally gregarious person, always enjoying occasions that allowed a little expansiveness of behavior. He was not worried by random meetings with members of the faculty that this occasion would involve. Informal commentary among the faculty of the meeting in his office the previous week promised them a concern with their complaints that was reassuring, at least for the moment.

Having arrived early, Beth Perwick chatted with the headmaster about nothing at all for a considerable time until Creston Langmuir entered the hall, when she excused herself.

Langmuir headed for the coffee supply by the kitchen and she met him there. "I'm glad to see you Creston. I think it's important for Board members to attend gatherings with the faculty."

"I'm more than glad to come. I always enjoy talking with them about our education program. Just the other day, I asked Dorothy, you know her, she's chairman of the math department, about when they introduce infinite series. She said they start in the ninth grade. I was surprised by that. I would have thought that came one or two grades later as it involves the difficult concept of an infinite number of terms adding up to a perfectly ordinary sum. But she assured me that the students do well with it at the ninth grade level. That's especially good, because the earlier they get these concepts, like that of infinity, the sooner they become accustomed to them, and are ready to move on. It provides the basis, of course, for calculus, which most of the students take before they graduate."

Perwick had to bring this kind of idle jabbering to an end. As they were standing apart from others, she asked him, "How is your faculty interviewing coming along?"

Langmuir spoke closely to her. "Theresa and I are done. We had our last interview — it was with Tony — yesterday. We thought it was best to leave him to last and let him answer his critics. We are prepared to report to the Board at its first meeting next week."

Perwick was ready. "I'm not placing this matter on the agenda for the Board meeting," she said in a sufficiently firm voice that her statement could not be mistaken for a trial balloon.

"What will you accomplish by delaying it to the November meeting?"

"Rather than report to the Board, I've decided the report should be made to the professional committee." When Langmuir made no comment, Perwick continued, "It's the best forum. Sometime next month will be appropriate."

He contemplated the change, "The professional committee is empty. It has no members; it has not met. It's a dead end. The report is to be buried, just like my bussing report. So Talent is still running things."

He offered to pass over it, "So be it, Beth," while thinking, "This change is not her work, so I won't argue it with her. I'll say little, and we'll see how much further she's prepared to go with this sudden change."

"With the committee, we can have a full discussion, don't you think?"

He answered, "Of course, Beth. I see nothing wrong with taking the matter to that committee." But his thoughts moved on, "Beth would never have plotted a move of this sort. She doesn't think that way. Talent will put some kind of small meeting into place, no doubt. With this change the Board at large is removed from further consideration of the faculty difficulties. And me with it."

Perwick was pleased to think, "That went easier than I expected it would. Maybe I can handle this job after all."

She spoke up, "For the Board meeting next week . . . on the matter of your academic committee," she continued, "That's something for you to announce, rather than my doing it. I'll introduce you to the Board as someone who brings to it an interest in the school program. Then you can announce the formation of your committee."

"That sounds easy enough."

Perwick thought, "Why won't he help carry the conversation. I'm left with listing things, and that doesn't sound quite right for some reason."

She finished her list, "When you want to take some matter to Tony, I think it best that I not go with you. You'll do better alone."

"Of course. That is what I expected to do, Beth." He thought, "Will these items never end. She has really been trampled over since July, and she's passing it on to me, presumably as instructed. Talent has been talking to her, and

11. A Third Resignee

severely so, to get this result. The friendly lady of last spring and summer is gone away. I wonder what he chose to say to turn her against me?"

Perwick was uncomfortable with Langmuir nominally agreeing with her no matter what irregularities she brought up. She made an excuse, "There's a faculty member over there I have to speak to. It's been nice talking with you, and I'll see you at the Board meeting next week."

"Of course, I'll see you there."

Perwick shuddered as she walked away, "Of course, of course, of course! Is that all he can say? What can he possibly be thinking?"

ANOTHER REMOVAL

Jacob Isaac arrived at the reception stylishly late. He had not been to the school since the June Board meeting. An annual family gathering had prevented his attendance at the July Board meeting. To his knowledge the school had been dormant during the summer. The field-grounds landscaping work that he heard about sounded routine to his ears, and nothing special about it had been mentioned at the budget committee meetings.

For the start of the new academic year, he was animated with his new role as an officer of the Board. As treasurer, he carried more fiduciary responsibility than other members and officers. He planned to master both the budgetary and the financial conditions of the school, and keep the data for both tucked knowledgeably under his wing. Isaac looked about the gathering. Bob Talent was not present; he moved over to the headmaster.

"Hi, Tony," he offered his hand. "I trust you had a pleasant summer?"

Taking it, Petrillo responded ebulliently, "Just grand. The family was able to spend the summer up-country where we have a cottage on a pond. We share it with my brother, but he doesn't have a family, so there is room for us together. I get up there weekends."

"Sounds like something we ought to do. We took the children on a car trip to relatives, but otherwise were stuck in town for the whole summer."

"Really," said Petrillo, turning serious, "I had heard you were away for the summer." Quickly, he pulled himself up short, thinking, "I regret saying that. It could get me in trouble. I guess Bob has been up to one of his considerable tricks again. So, Jake was not away! I wonder what that means."

"No, unfortunately," Isaac continued, "It seems that the children were so busy with things here. But that's over with, and this is September.

"Tony, the powers that be seem to have made me into a treasurer; I'll have to come up to speed. But I certainly want to do so without placing a burden on you or your staff."

"Daniel Goodacre is a very sturdy fellow, Jake. You won't bother him. Spend as much time as you like with him. Speaking of the devil, there he is over there. Must have just arrived."

On this note, Isaac excused himself from the headmaster, and moved across the floor to Goodacre.

"May I introduce myself?" he said, finding the accounting manager unattached at the moment.

"You're the new treasurer, I believe," answered Goodacre.

"Jacob Isaac, by name, but most people call me Jake."

"It's too bad you were away during the summer as a great many things happened. Whenever you want, we can get together and go over it, step by step. Just let me know, and I'll make time available for you."

Isaac had two decades under his belt as an accountant. He had worked at quite a number of businesses and partnerships in his time. He had seen an organization fall apart when the books were looked at very closely and some unseemliness was found. Isaac had learned to spot warning flags.

He thought, "Everyone was wrongly informed that I was out of reach. That, while much was going on. They didn't want me to see what was being done. Why not? Is there something seriously wrong in the school? Could there even be criminal behavior here, embezzling perhaps or, more likely, business being slipped to a relative at some inordinate price? Well, there is no time like the present to begin a step by step' look at the record."

Isaac was glad he had worn a three-piece suit. He pulled himself up into stiff professional posture, and looked severely into Goodacre's eyes. He spoke in an evenly tempered voice, "I'm concerned, Mr. Goodacre, that I should know something more right away. Could we step into the corridor for a moment?"

"Please call me Dan. Of course, right over here. Across the corridor there's an empty classroom we can use."

Goodacre led the way inside. Isaac swung the door closed. They took seats on classroom chairs comfortably rearranged.

Isaac opened with, "What are we talking about, Dan?"

Fortunately, Goodacre was equal to the occasion. Although he sensed Isaac's seriousness, he told his story in measured cadences.

"Last spring, it was decided to do a major overhaul of the playing fields. By filling in a gully — a very large culvert would be needed — and by moving the tennis courts, an additional soccer field could be fit into the available area. The

11. A Third Resignee

contractor would have to get it done between the last game in May and have budding turf for the first practice in mid-September. The scheduling was tight."

Isaac encouraged him, "Sounds sensible enough. Tell me what else went on."

"The contractor was selected in May. He required monthly payments, and payment in full when finished. Our problem was cash flow. We needed bank loans to cover the payments until the tuition money came in this fall. A concomitant decision was made last spring that we should change banks. In late June, we visited two banks and selected one. We moved our accounts to it, and secured the loan we needed. It's much more than we usually ever borrow, but we can handle it."

Now it was Isaac's turn. He had some questions.

"Were there, in your mind, irregularities in the selection of a contractor?"

"None whatever. We talked to three. The one we are working with was the most accommodating to our schedule and priced close to the others."

Isaac was suspicious. "Were you involved in the selection of the bank?"

"Yes. I went on the visits, met the principals, and participated in the evaluation. Everything was done according to Hoyle."

"Have the loans and payments gone through your hands? Do they look in proper order?"

"Yes they have. As far as I can tell, they are in fine order."

Isaac's sense of alarm was dissipated.

He considered to himself, "The usual opportunities for trouble were cleared as long as I can trust Dan. He shows no indication of nervousness or evasion; I'll go along with him, at least for now. Which leaves me with the big difficulty. What is the hiding about? Why wasn't I involved? Why wasn't I informed? Why no memos of meetings or decisions?"

He brought Goodacre into his confidence, "Why was I not informed of the meetings?"

"I don't know."

Isaac saw Goodacre was wary of this new area of questioning, and rightly so. He decided he had gone as far as was considerate of him.

"Thank you, Dan, for this impromptu review, step by step, of the events of the summer. Tony suggested to me a moment ago that I go over the events with you. We have done exactly as he suggested, Dan. It would be entirely appropriate for you, when you get back to the office, Monday, to mention to him that we had this talk this evening. He would be pleased."

Goodacre recognized the pattern of Isaac's comments, and was thankful for his courtesy.

"I will do so. If you have further questions about these events, please call me."

"Thank you, Dan. Maybe we should behave sociably now and show our faces again at the reception."

ISAAC'S SUMMING UP

The family of an accountant learns early that the master of the house occasionally gets pushed about by customers; it's endemic to the profession. Isaac had an "office" setup in the basement of his home for such occasions where the family accepted that he sometimes had to work weekends and evenings undisturbed.

The morning after the reception was a Saturday. At breakfast, Isaac could not bear to read the morning paper. His food did not sit well in his stomach. Afterwards, he disappeared down to his office, bringing a cup of coffee with him which, upon sipping, seemed to taste unusually bitter. He put it aside.

He had indeed been sociable at the reception after his talk with Goodacre. For the remainder of the evening, he did not contemplate what he learned from that talk. Its force hit him when he awoke the next morning: he was being cut out of Academy affairs by Talent. Well, maybe — he would have to go over it carefully to be sure, and he had obtained family clearance to spend the morning in his office.

"They visited two banks in June after the annual meeting," talking aloud to himself. "Bob, Dan, and Tony visited two banks. They met with the principals, the officers of the banks. They decided which one to choose for the Academy. They set up accounts, decided on signature requirements and distribution of monthly statements. It is unbelievable they would do something like this without the treasurer. But the Academy did not have a treasurer by title before I was elected. No one told the bank that the Board now had a treasurer officer.

"They secured a loan. They chose a contractor and signed on with him. This may have been done before the annual meeting. But, that just leads to the 'So what?' question. Was I not to be told about it?

"This happened within a few days of the election. Even if they believed I was going away for the summer, they could have telephoned to see if I had left yet.

"No, this was deliberate. Presumably, Bob let Tony know that he would take care of communications. Tony let Dan know. Talent remained the gate keeper. I was to be elected into fiduciary responsibilities, and then kept ignorant

11. A Third Resignee

of financial arrangements. Clearly, Bob Talent arranged everything. He must have planned it this way from the start.

"What to do? If I do nothing, I become a figurehead, but one carrying fiduciary responsibility. I find that unacceptable.

"The governance committee should handle this, but it is poorly staffed. In the several years I've been on this board, I have never seen John Stoddart do something on his own initiative. Greta Johnson is new, and very much alone. I would be face to face with Talent and without an audience to draw a judgement on the argument.

"Can I stand up before the Board and argue a list of grievances, obtain their concurrence against Talent? No, I'm not an orator. I would end up explaining how I really am a nice person. Or generate a letter to the members? That would get out, harm the school, and maybe land me a defamation lawsuit. I cannot do such things.

"But I cannot stay. I could resign the Treasurer's title. But do I want to hang around now that I see how the Board is run? The president is a figurehead; a member runs the Board! He does it by having put helpless people into the president's place and the GC chair, and by having gained the undivided attention of the headmaster. Why Bob wants me off the Board, I don't know, but clearly I am no longer welcome. These personality clashes are always irreconcilable. And I don't want to stay in a place where I am not welcome.

"So . . . , I will leave the Board."

Note 11: Shortened Terms

If asked, an experienced attorney will explain that once a trustee is elected to membership on a Board, it is difficult for the president to bring an early end to that trustee's term of appointment, and he certainly may not do so acting alone. That explanation applies only if the president follows the laws, bylaws, and customs that apply.

The governance committee carries responsibility for enforcing this behavioral norm. Our protagonist, however, has disabled that committee. Now he can shorten a trustee's term almost at will. We have seen this removal applied to four members: Jack Medford in chapter one, Creston Langmuir and Cator Blackworthy in chapter five, Jacob Isaac in this chapter. Of these four, only Langmuir has declined, so far, from accepting a shortened term. In each case, the targets persuade themselves to resign, not because of their humiliation, but because they find themselves ensconced among people who want to hurt them.

The president's purpose with removals may include a silencing of the Board, silencing a committee, eliminating presidential challengers, and eliminating one who plans to offer nominations from the floor at the annual meeting. Of these, each poses unacceptable risk to the protagonist, and calls for his best efforts to end that risk.

The protagonist recognizes that, for a member, sponsoring and passing a resolution calling for an election is difficult. If the members are largely unaware of what is going on, making the necessary speeches to explain everything to harness a majority vote will be a nearly impossible undertaking.

When a resignation is announced, the wise member will make a courtesy phone call to the resignee to say good-bye, and to mention how he has enjoyed working with him, and to wish him well. Because the resignation was a surprise, he should offer his hope that there is nothing seriously wrong, and then stay silent. Let the resignee break the silence. Has he an urge to offer a woeful story of unacceptable behavior, or not? There may be much to learn.

12. Cleaning Up

ANOTHER SETUP

The next morning Jacob Isaac called John Stoddart and in response, Stoddart made a pair of calls himself. The first was to Talent.

"Good morning, Bob. Beautiful morning for early fall, isn't it?" Stoddart began.

"Fine. What's up this beautiful morning?"

"Jake Isaac just called me. He was at the reception last evening, and he seems to have come away an angry person. He insists that he will resign from the Board."

Talent replied, "That's a shame. He always does such careful work. What happened, do you know?"

"It's about his new position as treasurer, Bob. Apparently school administration is not keeping him informed of what is happening, and he is taking his fiduciary responsibilities very seriously, maybe too seriously. I'm thinking, maybe he is not the right person for the position?"

"It sounds like you are right about that, John. Tell me, did he actually resign to you?"

"Yes. He insisted upon it."

"Will you please get a letter of confirmation off to him today? Don't use e-mail, John. That's too informal. He will want to hold a letter in his hand with your signature on it, to be certain."

"What about the Board?"

"You just announce it. There is no requirement to give the members an explanation. That would be inappropriate. If you are asked about it, you tell them that he left for personal reasons. It would be wrong for us to start stories running around the Board drawn from his complaints."

"Of course."

"Will you call Beth, now?"

"Yes, of course."

After a pause, Talent took advantage of Stoddart's call to touch him with another matter.

"You know, John, I have grave reservations about our new vice-president. He's capable of making snap decisions that have not been carefully thought out. He's also capable of taking snap actions that have not been duly considered."

"Yes. You mentioned that last summer."

"I want you to watch him carefully at his first Board meeting as an officer next week. He plans to have what he calls an academic committee. Well, as you know, only the president has the authority under our bylaws to create a committee."

"Yes. Is there something the matter?"

"Let's see if Langmuir abides by the bylaws. Let's just watch, John, if the president gets to announce the new committee. You and I will just sit back and watch to see how Langmuir goes about getting a new committee. Okay?"

"Sounds like the right thing to do."

"I'll see you there next week."

With that, they closed the call.

ANOTHER RESIGNEE

Perwick received Stoddart's second call. "This is John, Beth. I have unfortunate news for you. Jake Isaac has resigned from the Board."

"That's very bad, John; I'm terribly sorry to hear it. I had planned that he would teach me about the school's budgeting. What happened to him?"

"He called me just this morning and told me. He seemed angry at Bob. You get these things in management, Beth. It's a personality clash. Generally, there is nothing you can do about it."

Perwick tried a suggestion, "I suppose Bob stepped on his toes over something. He certainly has done that with me."

Stoddart assumed responsibility for soothing her feelings to help her in dealing with this blow, "Somehow Jake got his nose twisted out of joint, Beth. You can't help these things from happening occasionally. You have to accept them."

"I understand, John. I can live with it. Don't worry about me."

"I will make the announcement at the October Board meeting next week."

Beth had a problem with that, "What will you give for a reason?"

12. Cleaning Up

"No problem, Beth. Bob suggests that we explain simply that Jake has resigned for personal reasons."

"Okay, I'll go along with that."

With that, Stoddart ended the call.

But Perwick was upset, "Why does John call Bob before calling me. Who the hell is Bob! Does John think Bob is still president? If I could have a meeting of the officers of the Board, I might wean John over to me. But I can't do that because Creston turned out to be the wrong kind of V.P.

"Difficult."

A POLICY DEBATE

For its October meeting the Board met at the school in the evening. Talent had explained to Petrillo at their previous Friday afternoon conference that a discussion of faculty matters would come up and, therefore, the meeting would have to be an executive session. There would be no visitors.

With the second year of Robert Talent's hegemony underway, Board meetings did not involve distribution of minutes of the previous meeting, reports of committee activities, discussions of policy, nor were questions asked of the officers about Academy affairs. This meeting chanced to be an exception; one policy item simply could not be swept out of sight.

For president Perwick, in her second Board meeting, the resignation was the first order of business. After bringing the meeting to order, and receiving assurance from the secretary that a quorum was present, she moved to that matter, Robert's Rules of Order notwithstanding.

Isaac's anger at Bob, apparently for some slights he received over the summer recess, worried her. Even though Isaac was not present, she didn't want his anger and subsequent resignation to be discussed. She hoped that the announcement would go smoothly.

"John, do you have an announcement to make?"

Stoddart cleared his throat, and in his deep voice solemnly said, "Jake Isaac has resigned from the Board."

Member Walter McCarthy, a vice-president of Englemark Corp., raised his hand.

Perwick thought, "Just what I didn't want."

She responded, "Yes, Wally?"

"If I'm not mistaken, last June we elected Jake to be treasurer?"

"Yes, we did."

"Did his resignation have anything to do with his position as treasurer?"

Perwick answered, "Jake has resigned for personal reasons."

There were no further questions about the resignation. Perwick moved the agenda along.

"Creston, do you have an announcement to make?"

"Yes, I do, Beth," he started. "I'm forming a new committee. It will be called the academic committee. It will have members from both the Board and the school. The committee will be concerned about academic matters, especially academic development."

After this announcement, Langmuir looked around the Board for reactions and was surprised to see Stoddart staring at him with eyes as big as saucers. He could only wonder what that reaction was about.

"Thank you Creston," said Perwick.

Perwick moved to the next item. It concerned faculty complaints about the headmaster. There remained the task of moving the Board from the position she established in July when the Board voted to have Langmuir and Peterson do faculty interviewing, to the new position where these matters would be handled by her, Petrillo, and Talent. She had initiated this change by agreeing to hold that September meeting in Petrillo's office with the two faculty members.

Perwick continued the meeting, "You have met the Board's consultant, Talbot Train. He has been helping us with the matter of faculty complaints. I want to call on him to discuss the progress that has been made in the past month.

"Talbot?"

Talent had been diligent in arranging exactly what Train would say and for placing him beside Perwick. Talent placed himself remotely at one side of the circle of desks.

Train began, "I want to commend Beth for the diligence with which she has followed up on the faculty complaints of last spring. These complaints have been directed at the school headmaster. As you are aware, the Board addressed this matter at its July meeting. Interviews have been held, and they will be reported upon in due course. Meanwhile, I am pleased to report the results of a meeting held in Tony Petrillo's office with Beth, Tony, and two representatives of the faculty.

"The faculty complaints were thoroughly aired, and Tony has agreed to follow up on them. We, on the Board, will also watch to see that everything is done that can be done. I believe that this course of action will treat matters to the satisfaction of the faculty. And, therefore, that we can consider the concerns of the faculty to have been dealt with satisfactorily."

12. Cleaning Up

Perwick thought, "I'm surprised by Train's exaggeration of what we did at Tony's meeting. Talent did not bother to tell me what Talbot would say. Talbot forgot to include Bob's presence at the meeting, but I won't bother correcting him."

She picked up the baton, "Thank you very much, Talbot." She saw Langmuir's hand raised and called on him.

Langmuir had decided to speak up, "May I disagree? Although I was not present at that meeting in Tony's office, I am in touch with the faculty. I don't believe we have come that far, Talbot. We should accept that the matter of the faculty complaints is still on the table for our consideration and action."

Perwick was feeling expansive; she didn't have a thought that she might get punished for what she was setting about to do. She thought, "This is a time for me to offer something useful."

"I agree with Creston," she said. "We still have the problem. We really didn't do that much at the September meeting."

With that, the faculty problem did not get moved away from the Board.

The apparent failure of his ploy to manage the faculty complaints disappointed Talent. Petrillo was important to his policy plans. There was no assumption on Talent's part that he would be successful subordinating a new headmaster, if Tony was forced to leave.

He was annoyed with what he considered Perwick's headstrong comment. This outcome put the headmaster's continuance at the Academy in jeopardy, and with it and through it, it put his own carefully nurtured supervision of the school and school policy at risk.

The remainder of the meeting went uneventfully to its adjournment.

HURTING A FRIEND

While Perwick felt confident enough now to step on Talent's toes, she still felt bound to what she could do to prevent Langmuir from harming the school by some sudden and ill-considered action of which Talent had warned her. He had briefed her on a number of actions to take, and she had agreed to do them.

Before Langmuir could get out of the meeting, Perwick approached him. They no longer enjoyed pleasant chats about the school and Board. Since August, the Perwick he had known — a lady of straightforward thoughts and speech — now conversed in stilted statements, statements obviously derived from her talks with Talent. He doubted she was aware of how clear was the demarcation of the change that took place in August. To Langmuir, and maybe to others, she spouted detailed evaluations that were foreign to her own way of thinking.

"Creston," she began, "there are a couple of things I want to mention."

"Yes, Beth."

"You asked when there would be a meeting of the officers of the Board. I don't see how that would be helpful at this time."

Langmuir was not about to reveal to Perwick his thoughts or his reaction to her statement. She was only the messenger. Actually, he was somewhat amused at her attempt to play a power game. He was disappointed at this apparent decision to sequester him from the other officers of the Board. He knew, though, that since she had not made the decision, it would be pointless to argue it with her. In his view, she did not have sufficient standing from which to reconsider it.

Langmuir replied, "I hadn't remembered about that, but I'm sure it will be all right."

"Also," Perwick continued, "the Board agenda is full, Creston. You mentioned last summer you would like to make a ten minute presentation about independent school college entrance exam performance over the past two decades. There won't be time for that."

"So," thought Langmuir, "I am to be sequestered from the Board as well." To Perwick, he merely said, "That's alright Beth, I'll manage without the presentations."

Perwick withdrew from what was to her a risky adventure, "I have to see some others, now. See you later, Creston."

"Bye," responded Langmuir, but his thoughts drifted on: "How far does her awareness go? How far does her self-respect go? She certainly is aware that Talent is playing her to his own purposes, but she seems surprisingly helpless or indifferent in the face of it. Of course, our small friendship of last spring has disappeared without leaving a trace. Bet she doesn't know that yet."

Note 12: Heightened Awareness

Keep in mind how the protagonist obtains resignations: (1) by implying guilt; (2) by humiliation; (3) by giving something of importance to the target, letting him invest time in it, then taking it away in a casual and dismissive manner.

In the second and third of these, the mortification leads to two rather different assessments: (1) Why should I give of my time, talent, and treasure to the Board when they treat me so badly, and (2) why should I stay with a committee that has people on it who are willing to spend their time figuring out ways to hurt me?

For the typical member, a heightened awareness of what is going on is a partial antidote for the angst. Always note whether the Board leaders behave collegially toward each of its members. Is the GC disabled; are there sudden resignations; is there uncivil Board behavior such as, when asked, an officer or member stands mute and stares back at the questioner, and is there audible interference with speakers to prevent them from speaking or to distract the listener?

Always talk to a resignee afterwards to fish about for a cause. Regarding the individual member, is he seen as an activist that might threaten the protagonist's long term influence? If so, watch him. Does he think, speak, and move with heightened awareness of his particular circumstances? Does he suddenly disappear from the Board?

One of the most common types of interference warrants a detailed description including the minutia for which the alert member may watch. Placing a confederate beside a target to engage him in conversation as a manner of distraction is commonplace and the alert member must not miss it. A more effective version of this tactic uses two or three carefully prepared sentences with which the president introduces a topic to a meeting. The confederate placed beside the target has those same sentences in hand. This maneuver allows the confederate to engage the target instantly after the last word of those sentences has been spoken, and before the target realizes that the president has no more to say. By the time the target untangles himself from the confederate's conversation, the president has moved the meeting onto the next agenda item. By spotting this maneuver, the member who is mapping the Board can put several pieces into place without exposing himself.

To limit the establishment of a takeover, members ought not to resign. With an "us" versus "them" Board, it needs the member's insight, participation, and vote to eventually make things right again.

13. Coming of Age

STANDING STRONG

During the week following the October Board meeting, Beth Perwick thought about her conversation with Creston. "No argument; no strong words. That was easy. I'm getting the hang of it. Except I was too abrupt. I'll have to have a coffee with him sometime soon to smooth things over. He's a well-meaning member of the Board and has a strong following. And I mustn't forget that I want his introductions for Alexandra and Michaela next summer."

She tried to conclude her thoughts, "What can I do about Bob calling me almost every day? I hardly have an evening to call my own. Yesterday he argued with me that the Donovan boy should not be disciplined. That's a matter I discussed privately with Tony. Damn! Could he and Tony, in their Friday afternoon talks that were supposed to be about the contractor work, be reviewing my confidential conversations with Tony? That's outrageous.

"But Bob doesn't back off no matter what I say. And John's no help. Bob doesn't believe I mean what I say. I'm too nice to him. I'll have to insist."

About mid-month Perwick got a routine call from Talent asking about her plans for the November Board meeting.

"What does the agenda look like for November, Beth?" he asked.

"It's taken care of, Bob. It's ready to be mailed and e-mailed out," she responded.

"Did you include the Peterson committee assignment?" he asked.

"I'm sorry, Bob, but I do not need to review the agenda with you. I told you that it is done and ready to be mailed out. You will get a copy of it in the mail."

"I didn't mean to bother you, Beth. I was only asking."

Perwick was waiting for this moment.

She answered firmly, "Yes, you do. You do mean to bother me. You call much too often and when I ask you not to, you continue."

Talent reacted impassively, "Please, Beth. I only wanted to be sure that you included Papalian's report on completion of the landscaping field work. It was done on time and within budget. I think the Board should be told about that. Don't you?"

Perwick hesitated, "Didn't we do that in October?"

Talent spoke condescendingly, "No, Beth. Nothing was said about that at the October meeting."

Perwick dodged, "The agenda has already been printed, so I will call on Roger during the meeting."

But Talent was not about to let her go, "It takes little expense or effort to run twenty copies of an amended agenda through the machine and update the e-mails, Beth. I suggest you do it. Then your agenda will be done right."

"Okay, I can do that."

Talent doubled his bet, "Did you include announcement of the Summer Use project for Theresa?"

"Theresa. What was that?"

Again condescendingly, "Beth, you have to keep track of these things. We have to start the Summer Use assignment to Peterson."

Perwick thought, "Ohhhh, how could I have missed that one?"

"It's all right, Bob," she said, "I'll be sure to include it during the meeting."

"And don't forget to invite Tony's comment. I'm informing you that it has been taken care of. Tony has been invited to attend and to bring with him a member of the staff or faculty if he wishes. He knows exactly what words to say. Now, I hope your agenda is complete and ready for the meeting."

"I'll see that Tony has his say. Is there anything else?"

Talent closed the conversation. "Thank you, Beth. I'll see you at the meeting."

But Talent didn't want a confrontation coming at him every time he called Perwick. He decided that something needed to be done about her, and quickly. He set up a meeting with his three confederates prior to the November Board meeting.

CONFEDERATES KNOW BEST

For a late afternoon meeting of the confederates, Elaine Rutherford Blandley made available the library room adjacent to her office in her considerable house. It was far enough away from the Academy to ensure that they would not be seen together. There the four could freely discuss their personal interests and

13. Coming of Age

purposes at the Academy. Her two student assistants supplied them with tea and coffee. Talent brought the gathering to order.

"Let me thank you for coming this afternoon. We want to thank you, Elaine, for the use of your home and the refreshments. Your husband's position certainly brings with it fine amenities."

"Actually, Bob, it's not a very practical house. It's designed more for nineteenth century formality than for twenty-first century efficiency. For these times, it offers a lot of wasted space and the expense of heating it."

"Well, somehow you seem to manage it in style. Let me start our meeting by bringing everyone up to date on our progress. Pierre, you continue to be enormously helpful to me as chair of the budget committee. After Tony and I settle on the priority of various activities, I am able to turn to you to see that they are properly budgeted. These changes go mostly unnoticed by committee members. The only difficulty would come from Jake Isaac and, as we know, he is no longer with us."

Blanchard spoke up, "You are amazing, Bob. I really don't know how you do it. And maybe I don't want to. . . ."

"No trouble, Ruth. The member is given something nice; he is given a short time to get to like it; then it is taken away from him. Considering what he has given of his time, talent, and treasure to the Board, he usually decides the Academy isn't the place for him to continue with his participation, and he moves on. It's quite predictable.

"As for Jake, I can only tell you that, as usual, there are no witnesses, not even Beth."

But Talent wanted to get some work done. "The other party we should take note of at this meeting is Creston Langmuir. Perwick took an administrative and, I think, a social liking to him, although I believe there was nothing personal about it. That got us into a lot of trouble. She has accepted correction, but he is still in place and dangerous to us."

Blandley made a contribution, "He may be the smartest member of the Board, Bob. You need to be careful with him."

"Yes. That's why he is such a danger. Several members of the Board are vocal about him as a possible president. With him as vice-president, he is in a natural launching position. So far, he is well sequestered from other Board members. Our worry is that we still have a lot of difficult things to do if we are to successfully change this Academy. We need a couple of more years, at least."

De Vanough asked, "Why not put Creston overboard like you did Isaac?"

"He's more difficult, Pierre. You recall the episode last year when we yanked his bussing project out from under him. He didn't flinch. He seems to be too thick-skinned for that, I'm sorry to have to inform you. But we will be successful nevertheless. For right now, we have to keep an eye on him.

"In the meantime, policy for the Academy is determined by Tony and me, and that circumstance remains unknown to the Board.

"Next. We have concerns once again about Beth Perwick. She has gotten uppity again, speaking disrespectfully to me — wants to do things by herself. At the last meeting, she followed Langmuir's lead to challenge Talbot Train's report about the faculty. She was peevish with my review of the agenda for next week's Board meeting. If I let her get away with that, she will soon enough want to have Tony for herself."

De Vanough spoke up, "What kind of move are you thinking of?"

"I have in mind a verbal slap-in-the-face at the November Board meeting next week. That should help greatly."

Blandley asked, "Do you want me to do it, Bob?"

"It should be you or Ruth. At this point, it would not work well for a man to do it. Where you are new on the Board, Elaine, Ruth would be best. Are you willing to do it?" Talent asked, looking at Blanchard.

"I'll need some coaching, I think, but I'm willing to try."

Talent addressed himself exclusively to Blanchard while the other two watched.

Talent was minutely specific. "You get there early and wait for Beth to sit down. You go around the circle of tables, and take a place directly opposite to her. You watch the agenda, and pick a place as near the end of the schedule as possible. That way your show will be remembered best. You speak up in a full voice. That is something I want you to practice because you have a naturally soft voice. Don't raise your pitch, just make it a little louder."

Talent paused to see the effect of these instructions on Blanchard. She did not seem bothered.

He continued, "You speak up, loud. You say, 'Beth,' and pause to get everyone's attention. Then continue, 'I am disappointed in you,' and take a short pause. You say, 'you can't do policy,' and another pause. Next, 'you've not done any policy items this year,' a short pause, and a final, 'You're not up to your job.'

"The important thing is to not rush your words. Let each phrase settle in. After you have said these four phrases, exactly as I have shown, hold your peace. Stop talking. Say nothing more."

Blanchard responded in a steady voice, "I have that down. I'll memorize it, and practice raising my voice. But, Bob, what do I do if members start asking questions?"

13. Coming of Age

"While you speak, and afterwards, you look right at Beth. You may stare at her. If, afterwards, someone else speaks up, look straight back at them, eye-to-eye, but remain mute, say nothing; stare at them, but say absolutely nothing. Also, try not to show nervous tics: don't clear your throat, swipe your nose, rub your chin, scratch your head, and so forth. Do not lower your eyes until after the Board moves on, which it will do, quickly."

De Vanough asked, "Are the words severe enough, Bob? They sound a little bland."

"The words are meant to be palatable to the members. They will be embarrassed by Ruth's loud and rude behavior. They will be anxious to move on. Ruth's manner provides the necessary hurt, magnified by a room full of others looking on. Perwick will be mortified, but helpless.

"Any other questions about what we're going to do?"

They had no questions.

"That about wraps up our business."

As the four of them had known each other previously in different settings, but not as a group, they enjoyed a considerable time socializing about the various boards they had served on in years past: the city museum, symphony orchestra, churches, secondary schools, and colleges.

Talent was pleased. The meeting satisfied his need for purposefulness and fulfillment.

BAFFLING BETH

Perwick was still getting the hang of it. For this November Board meeting, her third, she made up the agenda herself, except for some unwanted help from Talent. No committee reports. No individual presentations. She allowed, to herself, that Talent had taught her well how to omit substantive items, because those invite discussion which can so easily "breed confusion." She liked the idea of avoiding confusion.

She found it easy to fill the agenda with routine items about the school, its schedule, its activities, its people, past and future. If a member of the school community got into trouble, and maybe into the newspapers, the ins and outs of it could be explained at some length to the members as long as the question of what to do about it had been taken care of. In this way, she planned to fill the hour and a half.

The Dark Side of Leadership

It was an evening session for the Board's November meeting. They met in a large classroom where eight tables were arranged in a hollow square. Members were seated around the outside of it so they faced each other.

Perwick opened with a strong voice, "If the Board will please come to order." Pause. "Do we have a quorum present?" Pause. Continuing from her notes, "I want to announce a new committee assignment at this time that will be of interest to each of you. Theresa Peterson's committee will do a study of possible rent-generating uses for the school's buildings during the summer months. Theresa, do you want to speak to it?"

Peterson was a long-time member of the Board and its most generous contributor by far. In previous years, she had led a survey of the school's college placement counseling program that resulted in its being considerably augmented.

Peterson was near sixty but appeared ten years younger. Her own children were long gone from the nest. She had a grand-niece at the school and was delighted to use her time to the Academy's advantage. She brought to the Board much business and Board experience, and was in a position to be generous as well.

She spoke in a full voice, "The idea with this program is to lease the use of our buildings to some institution or organization that needs space for a summer program. They could make use of the classrooms, fields, cafeteria, theater, and so forth, excepting only the stables and corral. Details of responsibilities, liabilities, and rent would be negotiated."

Perwick spoke, "Tony, you have been briefed on this. What do you think of it?"

"I endorse it. I think it is an important assignment, and I look forward to seeing the result."

"Thank you, Tony."

At this moment, Perwick allowed a considerable pause while she thought about what to bring up next. Ruth Blanchard, who was sitting directly across from her, took advantage of the pause. She spoke up in a clear, alto voice.

"Beth . . . , I'm disappointed in you . . . ; you can't do policy . . . ; you have not done any policy items this year . . . ; you just can't do policy . . . ; you're not up to your job."

At the rude challenge, the Board froze. No one spoke or even moved.

Perwick glared at Blanchard, thinking, "Aaugh! My God, what is she saying? Why is she saying those things? She's never said bad things before. We were talking just the other day. . . . I thought she was a friend. What am I going to do? Please, don't let me throw-up."

13. Coming of Age

After a long silence, Stoddart spoke up in a low voice, "Beth, why don't you proceed with the meeting."

The Board relaxed. Eventually Perwick found her voice.

"You shouldn't say that. Of course I can do policy."

When Blanchard did not answer, Perwick took a moment to ponder, "Things like this don't happen at Board meetings. Why do they happen to me? Why can't I just do the president's job and have things go along like they do when others are president? In three years, it never happened to Papalian or Talent. Others don't have these things happen. Stop. I better stop." Perwick realized, "If I go on like this, I'll start crying."

Perwick dove into her agenda, and followed it closely for an early end to the meeting.

Note 13: A Public Assault

Perwick did not know that Talent had brought Blanchard to the Board, just as she did not know that de Vanough, chair of the budget committee, continued to report to Talent. She knew not of the confederacy within the Board, and had not perceived an affiliation among these members. As a new president, she was taken completely unawares.

She cringed at the humiliation of the verbal assault. "You're not up to your job," Blanchard said to her. Those words rang in Perwick's brain. She had no way to understand why this should happen to her. She had never heard of it happening ever; indeed, it does not happen to others. "If someone feels that badly," she reasoned, "they would speak quietly to her first. Instead," she rehearsed, "I get publically mortified."

Perwick was also unaware of the transformation of the Board away from the collegial functioning, under Roger Papalian, to an "us" versus "them" operation under Robert Talent. She had not given enough attention to the sudden resignations. She was lost and completely vulnerable.

The previous spring Talent had carefully selected Perwick for what and who she was. We note, by way of example, that the GC did not even consider Theresa Peterson as a candidate. Had Peterson been selected and elected, she would have used the presidential powers for her own protection. Beth Perwick was selected for weakness.

14. A Member Governs

SEQUESTERING AN OFFICER

The morning after the November Board meeting, Talent called Perwick to get a measure of her reaction to the assault.

"I thought you handled Ruth's outburst with a degree of grace," he offered, assuming she wanted sympathy.

"I thought she was a friend of mine."

"Well, as president, you get different kinds of people to deal with. Under the circumstances, you did as well as can be done."

Perwick responded, "I didn't know people behaved that way at Board meetings."

Talent tried on an attitude to see how it fit, "I imagine she's frustrated over your difficulty with policy matters, Beth."

It fit perfectly.

"I know, but I'm doing my best. Should I call her and talk to her?"

He finished up, "Exactly. Re-establish a working relationship. Meantime, I'll give you some help with policy items."

He could tell she had control of her composure, so he went directly to the next purpose of his call.

"I want to have a meeting with John, Langmuir, and you next Thursday afternoon, if it can be arranged."

"What is it about, Bob?"

"It has to do with the faculty problem. Where Langmuir is an officer, I need to know his view of Tony, of Tony's abilities as school head. I suggest a meeting in the school conference room. The best way to get Langmuir's agreement, Beth, is to phone him and ask for an answer. E-mail invites contemplation. You want to avoid that."

"See if he can meet with us at four in the afternoon. If so, then you, I, and John will meet there at three forty-five. I'll call John."

Perwick noticed again Talent's complicatedness about arrangements, and it annoyed her.

"Okay."

"If he asks what it is about, Beth, tell him we are continuing to work on the faculty problem, nothing more."

"Okay, I can do that."

Talent turned to his last item of the morning.

"Beth, there's a problem with the new academic committee. It uses too many resources, too many people."

"I thought it was well balanced between faculty, senior staff, and Board members."

"Pomentare and McCarthy are two of the best people on the Board. We need them in other places."

Perwick argued against Talent's wanting to change so much of what she had done. In structuring the committee, she had followed Langmuir's requests to the letter.

Perwick thought, "Now he wants to fuss with it. Will his involvement in my duties never end?"

She asked, "Who will we put in their places?"

"No one. He's got a committee that's big enough as it stands."

Perwick was running out of gas, "Okay, I'll move them."

But Talent wasn't finished with the matter.

He spoke slowly in a low voice, "Now Beth, don't call Creston and tell him what you plan to do."

"No? How do I do it?"

"Just call up each of the two members and tell them they are moved off the committee. If they have questions, say that you are trying to even out the committee work of the Board. That should quiet them."

But Perwick still didn't understand.

"But when do I tell Langmuir?"

"There is no need to. He will learn about it soon enough."

She acquiesced, "That's not very nice."

Talent played it straight, "Remember our understanding, Beth. He is a danger to the school. We must constrain him."

"Okay."

With everything in order, Talent closed the call.

That same morning Perwick called Langmuir. He accepted the invitation to the meeting.

14. A Member Governs

ANOTHER SETUP

Langmuir arrived exactly at four o'clock, and was amused to see the others seated in place silently waiting for him to arrive. The only open chair was at the end of the table. To him, the scene had the false aura of a setup. He took the chair.

With Stoddart and Talent watching closely, Perwick opened the meeting by addressing herself to Langmuir.

Perwick recited: "We are continuing to study the concerns of the faculty. You will recall, at the Board meeting, we reported about a recent meeting with the faculty representatives in the headmaster's office. Central to this whole matter is an evaluation of Tony. As someone who is close to the faculty, Creston, we need to have your evaluation of the headmaster in his relationship to the teachers."

Listening to the long request gave Langmuir a moment to ponder, "What is John doing here? Beth is only a front for this performance; she would not even try to compose an elaborate consideration like that; she is merely reciting it. Bob is running things; it's obviously his request. But why John? He normally is ignored. As for my response, I have no idea what Bob will do with it. It must be a 'plain Jane' answer: nothing in it showing anything in particular."

He replied, "Tony fulfills the job of headmaster more than adequately, as his seven years in the job demonstrate."

Perwick waited for him to say more, but Langmuir tolerated the silence well. He just gazed back at her in a comfortable manner.

Finally, she had to speak. "Well, all right, if that is all you have to say, Creston."

She looked across at Talent to see if he had any signals for her. He didn't.

Stoddart made a contribution, "Is that all you have to say?"

"Yes it is," Langmuir answered. "I don't know what more you might want."

Talent signaled the end of the meeting by thanking Langmuir for his help.

Langmuir, on his way out, thought, "What a seeming waste of time. What could this really be about? Beth and John probably don't know either. And why was John invited? I think I played my hand as best it could be played without squaring off with Bob."

TURNING A HEAD

While it was the second year of his Friday afternoon meetings with Talent, Petrillo had not become more comfortable with them. He usually let him take the initiative when they met.

Talent opened, "The Board, Tony, continues to consider the complaints of the faculty. As I told you earlier, the October Board meeting decided not to accept my approach to matters, and not to accept the meeting we had in this office in September as a reassuring measure. The Board wants to do more, but has not yet decided what that will be. Your friend Jacobs continues to participate in these meetings.

"I met with the officers of the Board about a sub-set of this problem yesterday afternoon, Tony. As we discussed several aspects of it, Langmuir offered a statement that I thought you ought to know about. He said, and I quote him, 'Tony fulfills the job of headmaster most inadequately, as his seven years demonstrate.' I was surprised he would say something like this, but I have both Perwick and Stoddart as witnesses to it."

Talent was pleased to see the furrow that formed on Petrillo's brow. He mused, "I have succeeded in turning his head against Langmuir. That attitude might well prove fatal to Langmuir's ambitions should he ever try a surprise run for the presidency of the Board. And Tony would never try to confirm this item with the two witnesses. That would be too dangerous for him."

Talent spoke up again, "In another matter, I have what may be a difficult request to make of you, Tony, but I'm sure you can oblige. I wouldn't ask you if I thought you couldn't handle it. You're really a very capable guy."

"As the saying goes, Bob, I mean to please."

"You will recall when the study topic of summer use' of the Academy's buildings was assigned to Theresa Peterson, you nicely gave it your blessing. That is well underway, although I do not know how good, how thorough a job we can expect Peterson to do."

"Well, in the past she has done very good work on her projects."

"I know, but she doesn't talk with me much, and I don't want to take a chance on it. Here's what I want you to do, Tony. I want you to assign the same project to one of your senior staff."

Petrillo paused while he tried to swallow what was being asked of him. Eventually he replied, "To do the very same thing the Board committee is charged to do?"

"Exactly the same thing."

"Is that really fair?" he blurted out before realizing that wasn't the way to speak to Talent.

"You leave that to me, Tony," Talent snapped back at him. "It is not that big a task. There are only a few possibilities, and these can be put into dollars and cents pretty quickly."

14. A Member Governs

Petrillo ducked, "Mrs. Snow would be good at that kind of planning. She previously was a development officer for a large school that had some kind of outside summer use of the buildings and campus. I'll give the job to her."

"That sounds fine, Tony. We will need to be ready with the results in about six weeks."

"In the meantime, the December Board meeting looks dull. I was going over the agenda with Beth yesterday, and it looks particularly uninteresting. However, I would suggest that you attend just as a matter of appearances."

Petrillo responded, "Of course I will, Bob. I think that is important."

Talent went on to complete his otherwise innocuous agenda, and the meeting ended.

COLLECTING DATA

The day was the Wednesday before Thanksgiving. The school was in festive array. The morning was largely taken up with an all-school riding and other athletic awards ceremony, followed by a Thanksgiving themed lunch in the cafeteria and early dismissal.

Staff, faculty, students, and some Board members were floating about. For lunch, Langmuir chose to sit beside Richard Pomentare, a local dentist and member of his academic committee.

Langmuir opened with a jocular, "Maybe after my lunch I can choose a root-canal for dessert."

"No such luck. I left my drill back at the office." Pomentare rejoined. He looked Langmuir over carefully as though expecting something more. After a short wait, he decided to speak up.

"You know I have been taken off your committee?"

Langmuir hesitated, thinking, "I know I heard him accurately; there is no question in my mind about what he said or whether it is true."

Langmuir equivocated, "I was afraid of that."

"McCarthy was taken off too."

Langmuir refused to acknowledge his embarrassment, "Sorry about that, Richard. When were you informed?"

"Early last week."

Langmuir calculated, "More than eight days ago. . . ." He decided not to continue with the topic, "Well, I guess we will have to get along without the two of you."

Suddenly, Langmuir's eye was caught by Mrs. Snow standing over those on the other side of the table. She came around to him and whispered in his ear to come to her office when he was done with lunch.

When he showed up, Mrs. Snow beckoned to him from her office door. She ushered him in and closed the door behind him.

"You know, Creston," she said excitedly, but in a voice that was just above a whisper, "I was at the Board meeting when Tony endorsed the Peterson summer use project. Well, if you can imagine it, I have just been given the identical assignment. I'm to have it completed in January."

Langmuir was amazed at the news, but said nothing because the subject was too risky to allow an extended discussion. He didn't want to be responsible for a staff or faculty member losing their job because he talked too loud or too long.

After a pause, it was clear Mrs. Snow had no more to say. He moved back into the vacant school-office area, and returned to the festivities. But Langmuir was still listing the implications of what Mrs. Snow had told him: "Why two studies of the same topic, one done for free, the other by the most expensive staff person? And both endorsed by the headmaster? What could possibly be his purpose in such duplication?"

Langmuir had no answer to that. For the transfer of two members off his committee, he did have the answer. He recognized, "I am being sequestered from the other Board members. They are not to get to know me. More of Talent's maneuvers, no doubt. Beth doesn't think of things like that, she only gets to implement them."

But that wasn't what really bothered him.

"Bob Talent must have instructed Beth not to tell me about the removal of the two members. That's something Beth would never do; even if she did, she would never do it on her own. But she did do it. Bob's hold over Beth seems impregnable. Once again, she is no longer my friend. It would seem that she will do anything he asks her to do. I can only wonder what he has said to her to make it so.

"It's clear that Bob won't let me or the academic committee do anything of interest this year. Beth will help him keep me in a small box. Is it worth my while to stay with the Board, let alone as a vice-president? Beth will never call a meeting of the officers of the Board; Bob would not let her do that. But as for right now — I'm curious. I will stay with the school and its Board if only to see how this year plays out."

Note 14: The Uses of Untruth

Robert Talent in his second year of covert leadership moves quickly from his part as president to his part as member with special influence. His new part congeals out of five arrangements, listed in order of their importance: the careful selection the previous spring of a weak nominee for president; the counsel he offers her; the weekly conferences with the school headmaster; the actions he obtains from his confederates; and his willingness to tell each of them whatever will motivate them.

Perwick no longer believes she can handle her office without the continued help of Talent. She accepted at face value the small meeting of the three officers plus member Talent. There she heard Langmuir say, "Tony fulfills the job of headmaster more than adequately, as his seven years in the job demonstrate." She never learns more about this event.

Talent misquotes Langmuir to Petrillo as follows, "Tony fulfills the job of headmaster most inadequately, as his seven years in the job demonstrate." He knows that Petrillo would not dare to cross him by checking this with Stoddart or Perwick. Even if he were to try, the two officers might not be confident of their own recollection. Besides, Petrillo sees no reason to question what Talent has told him. Talent's risk of discovery is negligible.

After that, the Board would find it difficult to accept as a nominee for president someone from whom the headmaster was disaffected. This is a backup move in Talent's continuing drive to prevent the election of Langmuir as president, which event would scuttle his efforts of the past several years.

15. Another Removal

CONFEDERATES AT WORK

Although trustee activity quieted somewhat as winter weather set in and there was no Board meeting scheduled for January, Talent remained diligent. He started early at his annual task of providing for the Board's presidential succession in June. There were some substantial difficulties to be overcome during the spring that would take time. The possibility of the assembled Board electing a wrong person always offered a serious threat to the work he had done these past five years putting everything together and bringing it to its present state of performance. He would do whatever might be required.

Talent had settled his mind on the member he needed as the next president: a wholly presentable person of little experience and, in conversation, quite inarticulate. He had to allow for the possibility that Peterson, at the annual meeting, might nominate Creston Langmuir from the floor. Unfortunately, a comparison of his candidate with Langmuir would not serve Talent well, and might even be devastating.

In mid-January, he assembled his confederacy of Elaine Blandley, Ruth Blanchard, and Pierre de Vanough, at his home one evening. With the TV set rattling in the next room, they were ready to plan the spring's work.

Talent reviewed that they were all present at the November Board meeting, and only Talent was present at the December meeting.

"Nothing of interest happened at the December meeting," he explained, "although Beth managed to keep it lively with sundry items for slightly over an hour."

Talent moved to the core of their agenda today, "My choice of the member to succeed Perwick is Charles Durfee. He's harmless. He is surprisingly passive. He will be easier than Perwick to manage. And he is sitting on a lot of family money."

Pause... "No comments?"

De Vanough offered one, "How well does he pass inspection?"

"Just barely. But after Beth, he looks pretty good."

"Sounds like we can live with him, Bob."

"Let's move on. The important topic for this meeting is my concern that Creston Langmuir might be nominated for president at the annual meeting in June. He is a capable person who has a following both on the Board and in the school. As I have mentioned several times before, he is dangerous to us, and that danger is now compounded.

"Let me explain," Talent continued. "We have a considerable worry here, but from another source. Have you taken notice of Theresa Peterson, the chair of the summer use committee?"

"How could we help it, Bob?" answered de Vanough. "She is one of the more capable people on the Board. I understand she writes a check each year for five times the next highest contribution on the Board."

"That's true," said Talent. "And two years ago she came up with that parent survey report to recommend an augmented college placement support staff. It was implemented by the school. She is quite intelligent and, as might be expected in a late middle aged matron, she knows herself. That is, she is no emotional pushover. We have to be very careful with her."

"What's the problem?" asked Blandley.

"I had Beth assign Janet Whithers to Peterson's committee," continued Talent. "Maybe you remember, I once mentioned to you that Janet is willing to monitor and pass on to me comments by other board members. She's a lonely lady. She wants terribly to be useful. After she was so assigned, I asked her to let me know if Peterson ever speaks about Board elections.

"At the committee's meeting in December, Peterson mentioned that something was wrong with how the Board was being run. She said she would be tempted next June to offer a nomination for president from the floor in competition with the name offered by the governance committee. It is obvious that she talks with Langmuir from time to time. She might well choose to nominate him because of his support within the Academy. His election would be popular in the school as well as on the Board."

Talent raised the tone of his voice, "Ladies and gentlemen . . . we have to face up to it. We must do something about her. I would like to have you, Pierre, and you, Elaine, handle it, if you would, please."

De Vanough spoke up, "Do you have a plan, Bob?"

"Yes. Janet informs me the committee has a winter meeting next Wednesday. It will meet at the school at 7:00 p.m. in classroom number ten. For that occa-

15. Another Removal

sion there will be one member absent, leaving only three, one of whom is our Janet."

Blandley asked, "What do you want us to do?"

"You will attend the committee meeting, uninvited. Show up fifteen minutes late, so the meeting will be underway when you get there. You walk in, pull up chairs close, and act as though you belonged there. But say nothing until Theresa speaks to you, which, to be polite, she must."

"Then what happens?"

"You pick an argument with her by being critical of the committee's lack of progress. In the course of the argument you will use each of the following five phrases:

"You talk down to people and they don't like that. . . . You can't take honest criticism, you get angry. . . . You have become arrogant, you need to come down off your high horse. . . . Your committee has accomplished nothing. . . . You no longer qualify as a committee chair. . . ."

Talent was finished, "Those five phrases should be enough. Be sure to use each of them. And the last one comes last."

De Vanough offered his assessment, "That will bring her to resign, I would guess."

Talent responded, "Peterson, besides being intelligent, is a fairly rigid person. She's well to do, her husband is a trustee of another school in the Midwest to which he flies twice a year. Peterson has never even heard of the kind of encounter you offer her. She should take on an indignant rage.

"The next morning, her choice will be to call John or Beth. For their many years on the Board together, she does not know John well. Should she call him, John will not respond positively without instructions to do so. She most likely will pick Beth. Beth doesn't dare make a move without consulting me. Peterson will find herself talking to a lamp post, and with that it will be over.

"The last choice she has is to wait until the February Board meeting to make an angry speech to the Board. I have never heard her address herself to a group at length in the way that choice would require. I don't think she's up to it. If she should try, the two of you will be present to interrupt with counter-argument and quickly turn her talk into a nasty public food-fight that goes nowhere. In such case, you will not, of course, repeat those phrases I gave you."

De Vanough asked, "Bob, will the committee continue its work? Will someone else take over the committee? What will become of it?"

"No," Talent answered. "It would be best if it did not continue. We like to leave no witnesses behind, but in this case there will be the two members of the committee who were present. We don't want to provide a forum where they can compare notes and feelings about what happened.

"To that end, we have a back door on this plan. Should a question be raised about the committee's work, Tony has had one of his staff, I think Mrs. Snow, doing the same task. With her report on the way, Beth can justify ending the committee."

De Vanough was satisfied, "As usual, it sounds airtight, Bob."

"If you will be patient with me, I have one more item.

"You know Richard Pomentare," Talent continued. "He has been a member for two years. His sister owns the open land abutting the school's parking area where the school busses are lined up. As you know, we are quite crowded for land on that side of the buildings. When we last sold land for the Rolling Hills development forty-five years ago, we didn't judge correctly how the school would grow, and the amount of space that would be required for driveways and vehicle parking. For several years we have been making approaches to her to see if she might donate it to the school, but with no luck.

"Now the matter must be put to rest. To do that properly, the matter must be mentioned as a Board agenda item. For the February meeting, Beth will have three sentences memorized to do just that. After her words, however, I don't want discussion.

"Pierre, I need you to do what you do so well. I have Beth's sentences for you. I need you to sit beside Richard and talk to him so he does not ask questions."

"Glad to do it, Bob."

"The sentences are: 'The Pomentare land abuts the Academy's property. We have tried to persuade Sheila Pomentare to donate it to the Academy, but without success. That effort is now at an end.'

"With the word 'end,' you get to work on Richard before he's aware Beth has finished speaking. He's the only one likely to have any questions."

With that, their work was done, and, it being a dark, cold, and wet January night, they headed home early.

__PETERSON'S RESIGNATION__

Quite early on the morning after the meeting of the summer use committee, Perwick's phone rang. She was not expecting the call.

"Beth, this is Theresa Peterson," she said in a too-loud voice. "I've never been treated so rudely in my life. It was Elaine Blandley and Pierre de Vanough. Did you know they were coming to my committee meeting last evening?"

15. Another Removal

"No, Theresa. I didn't know that."

"They came to my committee meeting last evening and said terrible things to me. I've never heard of such behavior in my life. And, what's more, I won't stand for it. I won't stand for it for a moment."

Perwick asked, "Can you tell me what happened?"

"They just appeared. They walked into my meeting and sat down. They started arguing about things. When I tried to quiet things, they turned on me. I have never heard of something like this ever happening."

"Can you tell me what did they did?"

"They told me that I was not qualified to be a committee chair. They said the committee was not doing good work. Who are they to come in and say these things? They said it in front of the others. I've never been treated like this. . . . "

"I don't know anything about it, Theresa."

"Then I feel sorry for you. Now it's all yours. I'm resigning right now. Goodby."

"Ohhhh no!" but Perwick was talking into a dead line.

Perwick was flustered. While listening to her story, Perwick did not imagine Peterson was leading up to resigning. She considered her one of the most valuable members. What to do?

FIRMING IT

Talent received Perwick's call at his office.

Perwick was talking, "Bob, I just got an angry call from Peterson. She's resigning from the Board. Do you know anything about it?"

"Beth, what did she say?"

"That Pierre and Elaine came to her committee meeting last night, argued with her, and said nasty things."

"That damned Pierre! At times he can go off the handle, Beth. Wonder how he got Elaine to go along with him. If you want me to, I will speak to him about it; tell him to clear these things with you in the future. Would you like me to do that?"

"What do I tell the Board?"

"In an odd case like this, don't try to explain things. That would invite questions, and the questions would go on forever."

Talent continued, "You know, Beth, thinking about Theresa, when people serve on the Board for many years, sometimes their devotion wears thin after a while. Then an argument rises up, and they wilt; they just turn away from it.

You would do best to tell the Board that she resigned for personal reasons, and let it go at that."

"Okay, I can do that. I'll announce it next week at the February meeting."

"Be sure to have John send a confirming letter to Peterson. It should go out in today's mail."

"Yes, of course."

"Don't e-mail him, Beth. John won't see it until tonight or maybe tomorrow. Please take the time to contact him this morning."

With that, Perwick closed the Theresa Peterson account. She had not yet come to wondering what to do about the committee's unfinished work. Talent could not tell her about the identical work, nearly finished, that the administration was doing. That would tell her too much. He would keep that trump card face down unless serious questions were raised by the Board.

He took advantage of Perwick's call to open a new matter with her.

"May I bring up another matter, Beth?"

"Yes, of course."

For the last two years, I have been trying various approaches to Sheila Pomentare about her land that abuts the soccer field. She is adamant that she will not consider giving her land to the school. So the matter is over with."

Perwick responds, "Is there nothing more to be tried?"

"I think we have run out the string, Beth. So I would like to bring a closure to the matter at the February Board meeting."

"How would you like to handle it?"

"If you would say the following: The Pomentare land abuts the Academy's property. We have tried persuading Sheila Pomentare to donate it to the academy, but without success. That effort is at an end.

"Say only that much and stop. Say nothing more."

"What if there are questions?"

Talent wrapped it up, "I don't think there will be."

"Okay."

With that, they ended the call.

PERSONAL REASONS

At the February Board meeting, no questions were asked about Peterson's resignation. Afterward, Langmuir spoke to Perwick.

"Beth, why did Theresa resign?"

Perwick was ready, "She resigned for personal reasons."

15. Another Removal

Langmuir noticed how, as she spoke, her voice dropped to a low, hesitant note. He recognized this as marking another spoken untruth, of which he had noted quite a number during the past five months.

Subsequently, he called Peterson and, in half an hour, had the whole story of her committee meeting and her resignation. He accepted her story as a confirmation of his earlier thoughts about a possible confederacy. Langmuir thought, "This is not the work of a couple of unruly members of the Board. This event was much too big for that. It must have been directed by Bob Talent, and was aimed at me. Poor Theresa, too bad she had to take the brunt of it.

"I can only wonder," Langmuir continued, "at the extent of Bob's planning. Doesn't that guy have to spend some of his time earning a living? It must be a comfortable activity for him; second nature, and all that. He doesn't sit at a desk making up a list of the steps to take. He just moves through the necessary steps, delegating some of the doing to Perwick, Stoddart, and the confederates.

"Do Pierre, Elaine, Ruth, and Bob do this sort of thing for Boards all over the countryside as a continuing pastime? Is this how a part of society has always worked, unknown to the rest of us? And here I am, much too busy rebuilding a twenty-six foot sloop in time for summer on the lake to even think of taking up the Academy presidency.

"It really is too bad Theresa resigned. She was one of the best. Maybe we should have kept our Board contact secret? What kind of a Board would that be in which members work with one another, but are careful to keep others from knowing about it? This is not a collegial Board."

Note 15: The Eavesdropper

In this chapter we see the ruthless removal of a senior member from the Board. Besides making use of two members of his confederacy, our protagonist persuades an otherwise innocent member to accept assignment to the target's committee as eavesdropper. The ability to identify, approach, persuade, and direct such an otherwise uncommitted person is critical to a takeover operation. Our protagonist offers a superior skill at personal intervention.

To thwart such behavior beforehand, a member might offer a brief homily to the Board: To eavesdrop is unethical. The homily should teach members to report such requests to the GC including time, place, target name, and most important, the requestor's name. A forty to eighty seconds long lecture of that sort, delivered kindly and softly to the assembled multitude, may inhibit the protagonist from approaching an otherwise innocent member.

With Peterson's sudden resignation, if an activist member has spoken with her to learn of the nastiness, they should introduce a resolution: "Be it resolved that the Board abhors the insults expressed to Peterson, and offers its full apology to her." Since the members are not aware that anything happened, they will get informed as a part of the resolution's debate. The activist member, if possible, should have Peterson's statements of what happened to be read to the Board. They can ask the two confederates to explain their actions.

The force of this method comes from the requirement that a resolution, once seconded, must follow its course of discussion to the end, with each member's vote openly displayed. Aborting this process is difficult for the protagonist once two members get it started. It is largely for this reason that the protagonist takes strong measures early on to "quiet" the Board.

16. Moving On

LANGMUIR AND PERWICK

Creston Langmuir had now fully confirmed that Talent's confederacy saw him as a "them," and had been working to push him off the Board since he arrived there. He acknowledged to himself that his two fellow officers accepted Talent's insistence that they help to keep him sequestered. Langmuir's attitude toward them was necessarily ambivalent. He had expected to work with them in a collegial way, but Talent turned them against him by telling them disparaging tales about him. They both, in turn, seemed to be unaware of the confederacy, and were not suspicious of Talent's tales.

Participation on the Board is a charitable contribution to the Academy. In these circumstances, when a member is the victim of an attack, it is natural for him, even as an officer, to resign — his charity is not appreciated. From this perspective, to engage on this Board in political fighting constitutes an unanticipated and distasteful waste of time, talent, and charity. Resignation does resolve these conflicts, though unsatisfactorily. Langmuir, however, had an interest in the school that overrode these tribulations. But a call he received from Perwick one February morning undermined the understanding he had of his relationship to the Academy.

"Creston, this is Beth Perwick," said a soft and unassertive voice.

"Good morning, Beth."

"There's something happening that I want to tell you about."

Perwick paused for a go-ahead from Langmuir. When none was forthcoming, she continued.

"Bob is organizing a meeting, a large meeting."

Again, she waited for a response. She continued without one.

"He's holding it at the Harborside Inn, the one by the river next Thursday evening."

She waited. This time there was a response.

"Are you inviting me?" Langmuir suggested.

Perwick's voice rose, "No. I can't. I'm not invited."

She continued, "I don't know what's going on. He's got John coming to it, and quite a number of the ladies, and the budget chair, de Vanough, and Phil Penrose. It's quite a large number."

Langmuir was perplexed. He didn't know what position to take with Perwick. He tried to learn more.

"What's the meeting about?"

"I don't really know, but the annual meeting is only three months away, and Bob has talked also of setting up a search committee for a new headmaster. So maybe that's what it's about."

"Sounds like you should be there, Beth."

"I don't think he will ask me."

"It sounds like a rump Board meeting. If so, you can call off the meeting. You stop it from happening."

"I don't think I can do that." After a long pause, "John won't talk to me."

Langmuir responded easily, "I know all about that."

He thought, "This is a push and shove contest between Bob and Beth." He decided on his position in the matter, "I don't think there is a way in which I can help you, Beth."

Perwick thanked him for listening, and signed off.

In the weeks that followed, it occurred to Langmuir on several occasions that he may have missed a singular opportunity to turn Perwick around. But he finally dismissed these thoughts as daydreaming.

Only once did Langmuir hear again of that meeting.

PERWICK'S FOREBODING

Shortly after the time of the rump meeting of the Board, later in February, Talent called Perwick to request a meeting with her and some members of the Board. No reason was offered. She assented, and she agreed when it was suggested that the meeting be held in her home on a subsequent evening. The delegation would be Talent, and her chair of the budget committee, Pierre de Vanough, and Elaine Blandley. Perwick knew that de Vanough and Blandley had been involved somehow in the Peterson resignation. But, since then, Talent had promised to rein them in. She assumed this meeting followed from the Harborside Inn meeting of the previous week.

16. Moving On

Perwick's daughters were away at school and her husband did a disappearing act for the evening. They arrived at eight and Perwick had some refreshments waiting.

When they were settled in her living room, Talent opened his topic as gently as he knew how, "Beth, this will be a difficult meeting. While everyone on the Board likes you and admires you as a person, as you know there have been complaints. I asked Pierre and Elaine to join me this evening because they have been quite outspoken in their concerns with how things are going."

He offered a summary statement to her, "It is clear to much of the Board that Beth Perwick's performance is inadequate. It is worrisome to us for the reason that other members might be planning their own succession to your office. We want your resignation for the March Board meeting."

He made a full stop here to wait and watch how Perwick responded.

He wondered, "How spirited and imaginative will her defense be?"

Perwick answered, "I know there have been some complaints. Last fall Ruth Blanchard went at me. But there has been nothing since."

Talent had drilled his helpers well: each would spell out a serious complaint, Talent would ask for her resignation again, and they would hold still for her reply again.

Blandley interrupted, "I don't see important issues appearing on the meeting agenda, Beth. And policy topics seem to be utterly absent. I really don't think you are cut out to lead the Board."

The argument left Perwick appalled and speechless because it was Talent that had taught her those things. She did not respond.

Talent, seeing her shrink from the confrontation, offered a few soft words, "We know you have always tried hard to do well, Beth. But the Board's work has suffered and needs repair.

"Pierre, as I recall, you had some detailed difficulties that bothered your work on the budget committee, didn't you?"

"Yes," answered de Vanough, "On the matter of replacing the grandstands on the Lacrosse field, Beth, we needed a decision. You discussed the item with us, but a decision was never forthcoming."

Perwick responded, "I know. I forgot to get back to that item, but a decision isn't needed yet."

"Not quite," rejoined de Vanough. "Plans for routine seasonal work on the fields are well underway so we can get bids out in the next six weeks. That decision has been holding up the planning."

There was no way that Perwick could stand up to this kind of battering. She decided to give up.

"What is it that you want me to do?" she asked.

Talent responded, "So that the Board can move ahead, Beth, I would like your resignation, if it is asked for, at the March meeting."

Perwick could have cried.

She thought, "I had no idea that matters had come to this. No corrective wanted; just move out. It would be good to get out from under the endless blows I seem to suffer in this job. Nothing seems to go right for me."

The room was silent for quite a while. They were willing to wait until she had something to say.

She nodded, "Okay, I'll step down."

Talent picked up on that quickly, "That's the best thing to do, Beth. I know it's difficult for you, but you will lift a large burden off your shoulders with this change. I will bring up the matter at the March meeting next week. I truly think you will find this is for the best."

He changed to some light subjects for discussion that did not require Beth to find her voice for a while. After the air had cleared and Beth had regained her composure, the three confederates found their way to the door and the evening came to an end.

MARCH BOARD

Attendance at the February meeting had disappointed Perwick. Older members complained about going out on dark winter nights. For this meeting, when she scheduled it for early Saturday morning at the Harborside Inn, she promised them they would be finished by eleven o'clock. She was pleased to see that with that change, and a moderating of temperatures, this meeting brought a full house. Even Frederick Jacobs, the headmaster's special friend, who was now a local attorney, appeared for only the second time this academic year.

Thinking about her agenda, Perwick realized, "My position is up for grabs. Last week I promised Bob and the other members that I would resign during this meeting. But maybe today I don't want to resign. . . . It is amusing to think what Mr. Toad would say: 'That was a promise made when I was in a room with those three; now I'm not in that room any more. . . .'"

"Will the meeting please come to order. Please take your seats," she spoke up in a strong voice. At the same time she noticed how everyone was bringing to their seat a mug and a donut or pastry, and thought, "What a messy habit."

16. Moving On

"Let's get underway. I promised you eleven o'clock."

Clearing her throat, and still trying to stop the little conversations, she asked, "John, do you have an announcement for us?"

"Yes, I have." Stoddart put on an announcement voice, "Our member Theresa Peterson has resigned from the Board."

Talent, from his seat in an innocuous spot well away from the officers, watched Langmuir for his reaction. When there was none to be discerned, he thought, "Very good. Creston hasn't talked to Peterson yet."

Perwick was relieved at the silence. There were no questions. She paused before going to the next topic.

The next item was not on the e-mailed agenda. She had learned well from Talent in her short time as president how to avoid discussions. Substantive topics, when necessary, never go on the published agenda; they come as a surprise.

Raising her voice a little, and speaking slowly so members would pick up on it, she said, "As you know, the Pomentare land abuts the Academy's property. We have tried persuading Sheila Pomentare to donate it to the academy, but without success. That effort is at an end." She was quite surprised at the ruckus that followed.

Perwick wondered, "It's Pierre de Vanough and Richard Pomentare carrying on with loud guffaws. They're laughing together. How could this have happened?"

She almost shouted, "Will the Board come to order."

She glared at Pierre, thinking, "He's stirring up trouble again. But why now? And why with Richard while I'm trying to get out Talent's message?"

De Vanough spoke to the assembly, "I'm getting a consult on a molar that's bothering me." The Board broke up into laughter, and with that, the Pomentare land topic was over.

Talent was pleased, "Beth and Pierre played their parts perfectly. How nice to sit back and watch each of them do their dance."

But he had serious work to do. Ordinarily, Talent never spoke a word at Perwick's Board meetings. Perwick knew it would aggravate their relationship for her to cause him to speak by, for example, referring a question to him. He had never involved himself openly in what might be called issue discussions. He felt his time was best spent simply arranging to bring about the issue outcome he desired. Today, however, there was important work to be done that he could not delegate.

He raised one hand slightly off the table.

Beth responded, "Bob, do you have something to bring up?"

"Beth, I would like us to hold an election now. Do you have something to say to the Board?"

Perwick stared at him and remained silent.

After an extended pause, Talent continued, "You promised us you would resign."

Perwick held her silence.

Talent continued, "I nominate Frederick Jacobs for president."

With that, Jacobs stood up and recited a prepared sentence, "I feel very attached to this wonderful Academy and would be pleased to help guide its continuance." He sat down.

Perwick continued her silence.

Talent was caught up. He thought, "What can I do? She won't even speak. At the same time, she's looking at me. It's my circumstance. But, if she won't conduct the election, there's no way for me to move."

There was a long silence. With that silence, Talent's effort to bring about an election ended. Perwick was only stubborn; but that proved sufficient.

Perwick picked up the next published agenda item, and continued the meeting to the end, and to adjournment.

THE CONFEDERATES REGROUP

It was two months since Talent had met with his friends. During this time he had been unsuccessful in assuring himself that the next academic year would see his influence continue uncompromised. Peterson was gone, but Langmuir was still around and Perwick was still president. Many on the Board recognized Beth Perwick as less than capable and some might be thinking that an interim election was needed. When he selected her, Talent had hoped for a more seemly incompetence. His attempt to replace her with Jacobs, a respectable professional in his own right, had failed to his own considerable embarrassment.

He reviewed those events. "My rump election attempt was dangerous, even reckless. Fortunately, no one discovered I informed Jacobs that the Board had been told the previous month an election was to be held just as the bylaws require. Had Jacobs been elected, I could have led him about by the nose for at least a year. With Jacobs sitting as a new president, it would be easy to reelect him to a regular term without competition at the annual meeting. My mistake was to ask Perwick to resign. The bylaws did not require a resignation, but I thought it would be a smooth way to manage the change. I held her promise; damn her!"

16. Moving On

The four confederates met in Blandley's home on a late March afternoon. A student assistant was in the office next to the library room, but Talent had more to worry about than being overheard. If a truly qualified member were elected to the Academy's presidency, his four years of effort would go largely for naught. He felt he needed another two or three years.

With everyone assembled, he began his agenda.

"Let me thank you again, Elaine, for the use of your stately home. We have several matters to settle this afternoon. First we want to thank you, Pierre, for your excellent job at the March meeting. It was a marvelous performance."

De Vanough responded, "Maybe we should mention also your marvelous performance with Peterson. She was gone overnight, and with no repercussions. Congratulations."

Talent acknowledged de Vanough's compliment with a nod.

He continued, "Next, a bit of bookkeeping. Langmuir may have learned about the Harborside Inn meeting last month. That get-together served its purposes well but, if he were inclined to do so, he could challenge it in a state courtroom as an irregular Board meeting. To deal with that possibility, I'll have Beth tell Creston that she was the one who called the meeting. Actually, she was quite angry about it, where she was not invited. But if she called it, it becomes an ad hoc committee meeting. That should put an end to that possibility."

Blanchard spoke up, "But Bob, is there really a chance of things getting into state court?"

"One never knows, Ruth. If Langmuir gets angry, or if Perwick, for that matter, gets really angry, and either one figures out what is going on, they could move into state court to stop us. If Langmuir were to start saying or writing bad things about me, to stop him I might have to go there, or at least threaten to go there, with a defamation suit. It is important for us to keep covered on every point. Once Perwick tells someone, anyone, that she called the Harborside meeting, I am off the hook.

"Ladies and gentlemen," Talent continued, "back to our agenda. I have had one nice success with Tony. He loves Mrs. Snow because she never brings a problem to him. After much effort, however, I have his understanding that Mrs. Snow is not the right person for the admissions office. This will be her last full year; he will not renew her contract. We are engaged in writing a new job description for the search effort next fall. Her replacement will be a different kind of person. Her departure will be announced sometime after the admissions selection process is reasonably complete for next September's class.

"But we have a real succession problem with the presidency. I mentioned Charles Durfee at our January get together. I continue to believe he should top the slate at the annual meeting in June. I will introduce his name to the GC at its next meeting."

De Vanough asked, "How does it look for an unopposed election, Bob?"

"Dicey, Pierre. Perwick is feeling her oats again. I'm afraid she may want to bequeath her own successor to the Board. Because she is recognized as a failure by several members, they might want to take the election out of the GC's hands. We are about to look at both Perwick and Langmuir, to see what can be done."

There was no response from the others.

Talent suggested to Blandley that this might be a good moment for her student helper to upgrade their refreshments. After the pause, when they were alone again, he continued the meeting.

"We have to do something with each of Langmuir and Perwick before the annual meeting.

"Let's talk about Langmuir first. I will have John meet with him to talk about plans and arrangements for next fall. It will, of course, be an ambush. John will have a list of five or six humiliating things to be emphatic about. That will take some wind out of his sails. In addition, there is an outstanding topic on which he intends to address the Board. I have selected three ladies, including Janet Whithers, whom I will form into a Greek chorus. They will make humming noises during his talk to the point of distraction. The things I will tell those three to bring them into this activity will remove them as potential voters for him, should he get nominated. Three additional votes not available to him should prevent his election in any event.

"And, finally, a small item. At the school's Spring Fair this weekend, I will have Perwick offer to join our vice-president at his table, but put it off for the moment. For an hour or two Creston will see the Board leaders, including Beth and her husband, sitting together, while he and his wife will be seen isolated from them and saving empty chairs. This may put a little dent in his assumptions and inclinations as we approach June."

Elaine responded, "Sounds like you have taken on quite a lot there. On the other hand, the cumulative effect on Langmuir might be considerable."

"I think so."

De Vanough moved them on, "Are your plans for Perwick as elaborate?"

"No," answered Talent, "I just want to move Perwick to where she will have no thought of anointing the next president herself. For that, I want to ask you, Ruth, to go at her once more, just as you did last fall."

"Yes." Blanchard added, "That did go surprisingly well. I still don't understand why the Board doesn't react by going after me hammer and tongs."

16. Moving On

"They are embarrassed, Ruth, and, at the same time, they want to be collegial; they want to be nice; they want comity. Their response was hamstrung, leaving them ineffectual," Talent explained.

"Here's what you do, Ruth. At the April meeting, you accuse Beth of being a dictator. Let me repeat the instructions of last fall. Because it is important that you follow each of them. Practice raising your voice in loudness but not in pitch."

Blanchard spoke up louder, "You mean like this?"

"That's fine. At the meeting, after Perwick sits down, take a place in the circle of tables directly opposite her. Later, in the pause between agenda items, you speak up. You say, 'Beth, you are a dictator; you are just being a dictator.' Then you clam up; you stay mute; but you keep your eyes up and glued on those who speak until such time as the Board, in its embarrassment, moves on."

Blanchard was pleased, "I know just how to do that."

With the agenda complete, Talent moved the meeting to closure.

Note 16: Weakness Advanced

Giving responsibilities to members according to their weaknesses makes up an important part of this story. The source of the protagonist's proficiency, however, coming as it does from perception and experience remains outside the reach of this book.

The reader will recall from chapter one, that new member Greta Johnson says, "I sort of went from college into marriage and raising a family. I only had some hourly experience, but Mr. Talent didn't seem to mind. . . ." Not only did he not mind, he sought out that lack of experience to join it with her assumed lack of knowledge of the members.

The disablement of the committee would puzzle her rather than dismay her; this use of her, and the wasted service she offered would never become known to her. In her position as a member of the most important committee, she is quite impotent.

At the end of the first chapter, Talent explains his action, "The policeman is gone. No witnesses remain." The president enjoys an absolute confidence that Jack Medford, had he not resigned, would be, on his own initiative, a diligent policeman. Also, that his replacement chair, John Stoddart, on his own initiative, will not become a policeman, but will be quite content, even delighted, to join and support Talent in all matters.

In chapter eleven, they do not see the humiliation of Jacob Isaac as depriving the Board of his contribution. In chapter fifteen, they do not care that the tossing overboard of Theresa Peterson deprives the Academy of one-half of the Board's financial contribution each year. In chapter sixteen, they are not concerned that the assault on Beth Perwick deprives the Board of her good will and good grace. While these steps weaken the Board, they appear to the confederates to strengthen it. Never do they see their actions as hurting someone, nor do they see their actions as cruel.

A takeover rule recommends filling important positions with weak members, thus leaving policy influence in the hands of the protagonist.

17. Piling On

TELLING STORIES

Gone were the elation and confidence Beth Perwick enjoyed about her first and second Board meetings. Since then, the meetings continued at best in an uncertain and unmanageable way. She was pleased that she held her own position at the March pseudo election, but the event humiliated her just the same. She hoped the April Board meeting, now pulling itself together at the school, would be uneventful.

Perwick thought, "My agenda has only one special item in it. At Bob's suggestion, I mentioned to Creston that he should clear with the Board those topics he wants to discuss with the headmaster. He answered that he would like to speak to the Board about the absurdity of such a rule. Bob said to schedule it for the April meeting, so Creston is on the agenda."

Most of the Board was seated. Greta Johnson had sought out her governance committee associate, Robert Talent, and was leaning over his shoulder offering a candidate suggestion for the June slate. Talent gave her a quick response. Suddenly she straightened up to look about the room.

Langmuir had just entered the other side of the room. She hailed him loudly across the floor.

"Creston," she called, "Did you ever say, 'We are paying Talbot Train seven hundred and fifty dollars a day for his services to the Board'?"

Langmuir was surprised by this singular question. He could see that Johnson was standing over Talent. He realized, "She has just been told this by Talent. He's picking up on my several quotations of Talbot Train when he was introduced to the Board. In a statement, Train had said that his reimbursement rate is seven hundred and fifty dollars a day. By changing a few words, Talent now quotes me as saying something that I never said. Greta must have suggested me for the slate. Poor thing, she just doesn't know."

"No," he responded in a voice set to carry across the room, "I have never said that — ever."

Langmuir's answer bothered but did not surprise her. She turned back to Talent for an explanation. "When I looked at Bob for an explanation, none was forthcoming," she realized. He simply looked away at other distractions of the moment. I'll have to take my seat, but I'll bet I was told an 'untruth' as a way to put down my suggestion of Creston.

"I owe Creston an explanation for surprising him with a question shouted across the room. I'll speak to him after the meeting."

Stoddart and Perwick observed this repartee while waiting for the meeting to start, but had nothing to say. Perwick called the meeting to order.

PERWICK AGAIN

It was the custom now for the Board to meet without guests present. Perwick opened the meeting with a review of school activities for the spring, promotional information about the Academy's Spring Fair scheduled for the following week, and finally a reminder of the two remaining Board meetings for May and June. There were a couple of announcements to make, one of which was for Community Day volunteers to scoop ice cream for the school's public food stand in the village.

After these innocuous proceedings there was a pause.

Blanchard, who was sitting directly across from Perwick suddenly spoke up in a strong voice, "Beth," she paused, "You are acting like a dictator. You are not a good president. You are behaving like a dictator."

Perwick was aghast, "No, it can't happen. Why does she do this to me. I talked to her last fall. Everything was made good. This is awful." But she could find no words to speak.

The Board was silent and still. Everyone waited.

Stoddart, possibly the onlooker most put off by Blanchard's uncouth behavior, spoke up as he had done previously, "Let's get back to the agenda."

And they did; led by Perwick.

LANGMUIR AGAIN

Langmuir, trying to analyze what had just transpired in front of him, perceived treachery, "Ruth does not see Beth as a 'dictator.' She's playacting the

17. Piling On

part for Bob. He obviously asked her to do it. Beth doesn't know there is a confederacy at work — poor Beth. If I were to tell her about it, she likely wouldn't believe me. Poor Beth. Now I have Pierre de Vanough ominously sitting next to me, just as he did at my third meeting a year ago. I wonder what's up for me."

The Board soon came to the item that allowed Langmuir to rebut the suggestion that he should clear topics for discussion with the school headmaster first with the Board.

Perwick called upon him, "Creston. You have something you would like to take up with the Board?"

Langmuir spoke up, "Yes, Beth. Word has been passed about to suggest that before I take up a topic with the school headmaster I should first clear . . .

"What's that noise?" thought Langmuir. "There's a humming noise and oooh's noise coming from the group of three ladies over there. What is that about?"

He continued, "The idea is that it would be improper for me to bring issues before the headmaster unless the Board had first . . .

"That noise is louder now. Oh dear, we have a Greek chorus of three young ladies oohing and aahing as I speak. How can I continue with that noise going on?"

He looked about. Perwick and Stoddart acted as though they noticed nothing unusual. Only Talent looked fully at Langmuir with a curious look, to see how he would handle the situation.

Langmuir finished quickly, "There is no reason for an officer of the Board to clear topics before bringing them up with the headmaster."

As he finished, he noticed de Vanough watching him closely, "presumably to see if I try to make a speech about the chorus interference, and possibly about the 'dictator' attack, to explain how the Board is being run. If so, it is his assignment, somehow, to bring such an attempt to a quick end."

Langmuir was astonished at the extent of what he was witnessing, "What did he tell those three ladies to persuade them to interfere with me? In some sense, they must know it is wrong to interfere, but they were persuaded to do so. And where does he find the time and energy to manipulate so many people? It's plain that John and Beth think there is nothing that should be done about it. When the humming began, I should have asked Beth to call the meeting to order, but I didn't think of it."

"Thank you, Creston," invoked Perwick.

Whether Perwick knew of the chorus arrangement, Langmuir could not tell. He was deeply enough buried in the assessment of what had just happened to him, as Perwick was still engaged in what had happened to her, that the remainder of the meeting went by almost without his notice.

SETUPS GALORE

As the meeting broke up, and members were rising from their chairs, Stoddart came over to Langmuir and put his hand on his shoulder. Langmuir was surprised. This was only the second time Stoddart had recognized the existence of Langmuir at a Board meeting since he had become a member.

"Creston," said Stoddart, "I would like to have a meeting with you to discuss how things will be going in the fall."

Langmuir had turned about to face Stoddart. Glancing over Stoddart's shoulder and across the room, he could see Talent watching them.

"So this is yet another setup," he thought to himself. "Well, let me make of it what I can."

Answering Stoddart, he said, "Sure, I'll be glad to meet with you."

"I'm traveling during much of April, how about mid-May?"

"I don't know, John. May's bad for me. How about a time in mid-June after we're done with our Board duties for the year?"

"Oh no! We have to fit it in before that. Let's get our schedule books out to see what can be done."

Langmuir was pleased. He thought, "I sleuthed that one out. The topic is not about next fall. It's about the June annual meeting."

Stoddart spoke, "Here is a date. Maybe we could have breakfast?"

"I'm clear on that date. I'll see you then for breakfast."

As John marched off, his duty done, Langmuir saw the room had cleared, except that Greta Johnson was walking toward him.

"Creston," she called. "Wait, I want to speak with you."

"I'm sorry," she began when she reached him. "I didn't mean to put you on the spot with my question. I really didn't know what to do."

"What's the matter, Greta?" he sympathized.

"It's the strange way the governance committee works, Creston. They are considering Charles Durfee for the slate in June. I see him at meetings and he doesn't seem to be an interesting person. So, before this meeting began, I suggested your name to Bob. He said you were a rumormonger and quoted you. I sensed the quote was manufactured for the moment, and that's why I asked you about it."

"Well, Greta, I am glad to confirm your doubts."

17. Piling On

"Sometimes," she said softly, "I don't know why I'm on that committee, because I don't know the people they are talking about." She added, "John says nothing. He never has a suggestion of what to do."

Hearing her confession, Langmuir felt sorry for her. "I know," he said, "but maybe things will work out all right just the same."

She smiled, and replied, "Maybe so. Thank you."

The room was otherwise empty. They went off to their cars.

A MEETING FOR TWO

When Langmuir arrived at the Inn for the breakfast meeting with Stoddart at the agreed hour of nine o'clock, he found him sitting at a small, square table pushed against a wall with Stoddart seated facing the wall, which left an open place on either side. He noted that Stoddart was deep into his breakfast, another case of Langmuir arriving on time only to find that others were at work fifteen minutes earlier.

"Good morning, John," said Langmuir quietly as he took the chair on Stoddart's left side, and placing them too close to each other for Langmuir's comfort.

"Good morning, Creston. I'm on a tight schedule this morning. I hope you'll excuse me for going ahead with my breakfast."

"Not at all, John."

The waitress came up, and asked Langmuir if he wished to order.

To the waitress, "I'll only have coffee, please."

Stoddart spluttered and stared at Langmuir, "Huh. What's that? You're not going to join me?"

Langmuir repeated himself, "Coffee only will do."

They talked about the fine spring weather for a minute or so until the coffee was brought and the waitress gone.

Stoddart backed off from his food, sat up straight, wiped his lips well with his cloth napkin, composed himself, and turned at the hip so that his whole upper body was facing Langmuir. The small table brought them close together — head to head.

Stoddart said firmly, "You will never be president." He paused momentarily. Then went on, "If you are a committee chairman, it will only be for a subcommittee." Pause, "You will not meet any more with the school headmaster. You will not be given important Board assignments. You will not have a place in the Board leadership again."

Langmuir pulled a note pad out of his jacket pocket and noted down on it the list Stoddart had pronounced. As he was writing, he noticed, "John has greatly relaxed and returned to his food. For him the remainder time gets devoted to soothing me, so I will take the ambush in good humor. It's Bob that wants me off the Board, but John does not understand this. He takes the list he was given literally. That it might anger me into jumping ship, John recognizes as a danger, not as an opportunity.

"That finishes the idea of this being a discussion meeting," thought Langmuir. "The list is not John's, so there is no point in trying to discuss it with him. He talks to nobody unless ordered to do so, as now. He is unaware of the existence of the confederacy, and that sometimes members get pushed overboard. We have nothing to talk about."

Stoddart tried to continue with his duties, "We can talk about how things will be arranged for the fall, Creston."

"But are you not retiring from the Board this June?"

"Yes, I am."

Langmuir drilled right in, "If I wanted to talk about the fall, wouldn't it be best for me to talk with Beth?"

"Can't you be collegial, Creston? I'm offering to help you."

Langmuir got very collegial, "Let's talk about who will be on the slate for the next president."

"I think that would be inappropriate. That is a matter for the governance committee."

"Not very collegial, John," said Langmuir. He thought, "Let's see how Greta's nominee works with John."

"Charles Durfee goes on the slate, does he not John?"

Stoddart wanted to sooth Langmuir into remaining on the Board. To do this he had to talk to him until he got over the initial shock of the ambush. He wanted Langmuir to leave the restaurant calmed. Durfee would have to serve for conversation.

Stoddart amplified, "I realize that the headmaster, or a new headmaster, will have Anne Durfee reporting to him, and that he will be reporting to Charles Durfee as president of the Board. The committee allows this as an acceptable arrangement, Creston."

Now Langmuir knew for sure that the nominee on the official slate would be Durfee for president.

"Your Committee, John, such as it is, needs an independent mind on it. That nomination is absurd. It puts the headmaster in an impossible position. There is no way to alleviate the situation. That can't work."

17. Piling On

Stoddart didn't like Langmuir's innuendo about the inadequacy of his committee, nor his articulate stand against the nominee. He would have to find an easier topic for them.

"Well, I'm sorry you see it that way, Creston. What would you like to do on the Board in the fall? How would you like to fit in?"

With that, Langmuir stood up. He collected his note pad, pen, and glasses from the table, and put a full-sized tip under his plate for the waitress.

"Huh, what's that . . . I haven't finished my breakfast. We were to talk."

"John, you and I have nothing to talk about. Good day."

Langmuir left the table and the Inn. Driving home he became aware that there was no real purpose to be served by his staying longer on the Board.

Note 17: Spontaneous Response

Spontaneous response requires a practiced skill. The knowledgeable member watched the election attempt at the March Board meeting well aware of the required one month notification omission. Also, as that member watched Ruth Blanchard attack Beth Perwick, he realized Blanchard's complaint was artificial, made the assumption it was Talent's doing, and concluded that it purposely subjugated Perwick further by means of a public humiliation.

How does one respond to either of these events spontaneously without defaming another member? In the attempted irregular election, wait until the event is complete. Point out how an irregular election might necessarily revert to the state courts to resolve the resulting mess, how uncertain the outcome must be, and how such reckless behavior is dangerous to the continuance of the Academy.

With the attack, one may take a most natural course if embarrassment over the episode can be set aside quickly. Question Blanchard about her concerns. Encourage her to fully explain her complaint to the Board. It may turn out that she cannot describe any concern; she may even refuse to speak. If there is no report of an ongoing complaint, then she most likely contrived the attack. Speak of Blanchard's sponsorship to the Board by Talent. Ask Talent if there is a connection between them, and if they planned this assault together. In this way, inform the members, especially the president, of possible insidious behavior.

If Blanchard and Talent respond with incivility by refusing to speak, make that incivility a topic of discussion. Move on to express a possible need for new leadership through open elections, especially at the annual meeting. A member can bring up this mentioning of open elections at the annual meeting repeatedly.

18. Harassment

THE MAY BOARD

Beth Perwick never recovered from the April "dictator" assault. Her elation at thwarting a rump election in March dissipated under the attack. To see her way through the May and June meetings, she carefully coordinated her every move with Talent.

As the May Board gathered, she mused about these difficulties, "Bob seems to have the real management skills around this place. Only with him in the loop did things go well for at least a month at a time. People can be so difficult: Pierre and Elaine's argument with Theresa causing her to leave; then there was Ruth coming at me personally, and twice, and at Board meetings in front of everyone. I didn't know people behaved like that.

"I thought that the office of president would be much more a matter of just doing what needed to be done. But that didn't work. At least I've kept the job through June, a full year. I wonder how Charles Durfee will do next year. Well, let's get going."

She addressed the members, "Will the Board please come to order."

While Perwick led the Board through the usual pablum agenda, Langmuir continued to figure out how the Board was managed — to explain the strange moves that occurred.

Langmuir analyzed the past two meetings, "Bob sure does hammer on an innocent like Beth. There were two accurately staged assaults on her, and they devastated her. But she would not call a meeting of the officers where a subject like this could be developed and set forth.

"Beth alone would not believe me, or at best would be thoroughly confused. John would not risk believing me. He is well committed to helping Bob keep me down and will not talk with me. The difficulty here is to get my head out of the collegiality box, and start thinking about 'us' versus 'them' as the operating mode of the Board, in which I am a 'them.'

"It is amusing to watch Bob at the meetings. He sits off to one side, never near an officer or a confederate. Since the last annual meeting, he has not said a single word, except for the faux election last month. He just watches as his words are spoken and his plans enacted. But what an enormous time he puts in to accomplish that. His imposition of some unknown policy upon the school must be awfully important to him.

"The latest event was Beth offering to sit with me and Sally at the Spring Fair, and then, while we held chairs for her, she and Steve sat with John, Bob, and Tony, and their wives. It was obviously staged, and the sort of thing Bob would do, but not something Beth would think of. Always embarrass and sequester the target, these are the two themes that Talent applies over and over again: embarrass and sequester.

"I have to pay attention," Langmuir realized, "back to the meeting. Let me raise a point that needs airing about the Durfee nomination."

At a pause in Perwick's agenda, he raised his hand.

"Yes, Creston."

"I have a concern with what I have heard about a possible nomination for our next president."

Langmuir heard a gasp from the direction of Talent.

He continued, "Charles Durfee, it seems, is on the GC's election slate for next month for the office of president."

Langmuir paused to slow his delivery. He wanted the Board to follow what he had to say.

"Charles is a fine candidate and would make a good president under ordinary circumstances. I would support his candidacy." Pause . . .

"I should point out though that Anne Durfee, as we know, is head of the middle school. In this position she reports directly to the school headmaster." Pause . . .

"Were Charles to be elected president of the Board, the school headmaster would report to him, in effect." Pause . . .

"This arrangement would be like a sandwich, with the school headmaster as the filling placed between two slices of bread in the persons of Charles and Anne Durfee." Pause . . .

"I understand, we understand, that the parties to such an arrangement may agree to be on their best behavior and act independently in their duties. And I'm sure they would try to do so, in good faith." Pause . . .

"But it is still the wrong thing to do. It puts the headmaster of the school in a thoroughly compromised position to have reporting to him the wife of the person to whom he reports." Pause . . .

18. Harassment

"Such an arrangement is so bad, they don't even write management articles about avoiding it. Everyone knows instinctively that it's wrong. So let's not put Charles into that position."

When he finished speaking, there was a long silence that spread across the Board. Most of those other members who at one time might have added to Langmuir's remarks, had been, by one means or another, induced to resign. The silence was complete.

A capable host might speak up to defer further commentary to the next Board meeting where, during the election process, discussion of qualifications and circumstances of the candidates would be more appropriate, even if such comment served as a rebuke to Langmuir, but Talent had cautioned Perwick against using the word "election" during this meeting, and the Board did not have a capable president.

Eventually Perwick picked up the floor presence, returned to the comfort of her agenda, and reminded members that the next meeting was the Board's annual meeting. She had wanted to mention that "annual" meeting meant election of the next Board president, but that was forbidden.

Nothing more of interest happened at the May meeting, and the meeting itself was soon over.

ANGER

Talent and Perwick met in an empty classroom at the Academy the next day. Talent was in a fury. He had called Perwick late the previous evening, after the Board meeting, to ask for them to meet this morning.

As he closed the door behind him, he turned to Perwick and spoke angrily at her, "I will not let that bastard undo the work I have done."

Perwick was relieved. While he was speaking angrily at her, he was not angry with her. He was in a rage over Langmuir.

Talent toned himself down a bit, "He has undone what the governance committee so carefully prepared in its selection of Durfee."

Perwick calmed him further, "No one responded to what he said, Bob. We can go ahead with our plans for Durfee regardless. Can't we?"

"No. I think not. His argument is too substantial. As long as it was bottled up in the GC, we could ignore it for the election. After that, it would simply be 'too bad, we didn't think of it.' But not now that it has been exposed to the whole Board."

"I see," said the president. "What do we do about it?"

"First, we fix Langmuir."

"Oh? What do you mean?"

"He's got to go," said Talent.

"What do you mean? Go where?"

To speed up the process, Talent took a new step with Perwick. He thought, "Beth has come far enough in the past year that I can reveal the last increment to her."

As casually as he knew how, he said, "We have to remove him from the Board."

"Can we do that?" she asked.

Talent thought, "Oh dear, what did I say?"

"Beth, we will threaten to put him on trial. If he stays, we will put him on trial."

"Is that done?"

"I think so. I'll have to look up the procedure. But in the meantime, Beth, call him to meet with us in the school conference room early next week."

"What will I tell him?"

"You and I want to talk to him. That will do."

Perwick was uncomfortable with that. She could imagine an argument, but she was willing to try.

Talent moved to the second item, "Beth, there is the matter of coming up with a new candidate. I want you to remove Greta Johnson from the GC, and replace her with Barbara Antlower."

"Is she good?"

Talent brought her along, "She's okay. I worked with her setting up the Greek chorus to annoy Langmuir at the April Board."

"But should she be on the GC? How do you tell?"

Here Talent's frustration with how badly things were going showed. He slipped up again, "She's new on the Board, right out of college into family raising, and she's never worked on a salary job."

Perwick stared at Talent, "What's that got to do with it?"

He backtracked as best he could, "Actually nothing. But I could tell she would do well on the committee. Please make the change next week, so she will be sitting on it at its last meeting in late May."

"Okay, Bob. But what are we going to do for a new candidate?"

"I'm working on it. That's all I have for now, Beth. Let me know as soon as you contact Langmuir."

With that, they were done.

18. Harassment

THE DENOUEMENT

Langmuir agreed to a meeting with Talent and Perwick at her request. He knew better, but he still held to vain hopes. He did, however, inform Perwick that he would bring another member with him to witness the proceedings. She hesitated about that, but did not argue with him. The meeting was set for the school's small conference room.

Langmuir asked member Richard Pomentare, whose Board experiences the two of them had discussed, to join him. This proved to be an unfortunate selection. He was simply not up to the emotional burden of such a meeting.

Langmuir and Pomentare arrived at the appointed time only to find that Talent and Perwick were positioned on either side of the small table. They were turned sideways to it so their feet took up the available space. They invited Pomentare to take a place at the further end. At the near end of the table, the only remaining chair and space awaited Langmuir.

As he took his seat, Talent leaned over at him and quietly said in his ear, "We are invoking the 'tabling' procedure."

Langmuir acknowledged this statement, but Pomentare was waiting for the meeting to begin. He did not hear it, and did not notice that he had missed something.

To open the meeting, Talent began, "The Board was informed during the spring season a year ago that there was faculty anger with the headmaster. So the special meeting last July about these difficulties was not a surprise to the Board."

Langmuir had to think his way through the diversion, "I was aware that, as a V.P. I had generated a memo for the Board pointing out that the Board was surprised by the faculty attitude when informed of it at the special July Board meeting. Bob's statement was simply not true; there had been no such informing of the Board. He could see no connection with that and the matter that brought this meeting together, namely, his statement about Durfee's candidacy at last week's Board meeting."

Talent picked up another seemingly irrelevant point, "Beth, last October, when you removed two members from the academic committee, why did you remove them?"

"I moved them off the academic committee because their skills were needed on other committees," responded Perwick as she stretched out her legs and stared at the tops of her shoes.

Langmuir thought to comment about the only too obvious state of her conscience, but held back because he didn't see where the meeting was going.

Talent moved in, "Creston, you are not abiding by the rules of the Board. I am considering opening a series of charges against you. Beth, will you read the list to Creston, please."

As Perwick lifted up the writing pad in front of her, Langmuir noticed, "The list is handwritten. But Beth never learned how to write, that is, she never learned cursive writing. I've watched her for a couple of years as a member of the Board. She can only print in block letters, and those tend to drift above and below the line. Whose list is that? It's probably Bob's, but I can't be sure."

Perwick read, "Langmuir failed to follow instructions concerning his visits to the headmaster of the school. He has failed to give direction to his academic committee. He has brought confidential matters to the attention of the full Board. . . ."

Langmuir listened in disbelief to the items. He thought, "Isn't this too clever. What I said last week, while it is the cause of what is taking place here, will not be discussed. Instead, Bob will just open up a new front in his war. And look at my 'witness' at the other end of the table. Richard had buried his head in his arms on the table. He could not tolerate watching such antagonistic proceedings. My wrong choice."

He spoke up, "This list is foolishness. If you have something against me, you have to type it up, sign it, both of you, and send me a copy. Otherwise, you have nothing."

Talent, to Langmuir's surprise, adjourned the meeting. He and Perwick left promptly. Langmuir gathered up Pomentare and they headed out of the building in the direction of the parking lot.

When they were clear of the building, Pomentare spoke, "That was awful, Creston."

"I know, but that's what has become of it."

"Bob said that the Board was warned about faculty attitudes last spring. That's not so. We were completely surprised by it in July."

"Again, I know that, Richard. I have heard Bob say things of that sort ever since I joined the Board."

"But why did he say it?"

"I don't know. I would guess that to some extent its compulsive with him." They had reached the parking lot.

Pomentare said, "Bye, Creston, sorry I couldn't be of more help to you."

"Bye, Richard. Thank you for coming."

With that they parted ways to head each for his car.

As Langmuir walked toward his, however, he heard someone holler his name, "Who the hell could be hollering at me out here. There he is coming

18. Harassment

from the school. It's Bob Talent. He's almost running. What can he want with me now?"

Talent pulled up, "Creston!"

"Hello."

"I had to talk with Beth after the meeting." Talent said, "Then I looked for you. I'm glad I was able to find you."

"What do you want?"

Talent slowed and took a deep breath, "I want you to understand, Creston, that I plan to continue with this matter. You should understand that it could be very embarrassing for you."

"I'm not easily embarrassed, Bob."

"Please keep what I have said in mind. Good bye."

With that, Talent walked back toward the school.

Langmuir looked for his car: "Imagine him following Richard and me until Richard left and I was alone. Only then does he deliver the intimidation. That was probably the purpose of the meeting in the first place.

"I made two mistakes. I should have insisted with Beth that I would only meet with the governance committee. That would have involved Greta as another witness; speaking of which, I should have been more thoughtful in picking a witness to bring with me."

Getting into his car he had a final thought, "How long do I want to keep up this contest? Maybe I've gone as far as it's worth going."

Note 18: Working Outside the Box

After two years of trying, we have here the defeat of Creston Langmuir, who is not prepared to endure the threat of a general condemnation by whatever means Talent may gin up.

In these circumstances, members must be mindful that the protagonist has several committed confederates willing to swear, in support of one another, to statements they heard Langmuir make. Langmuir, on the other hand, will have no success persuading other Board members, by way of helping him, to face an aggressive cross examination. He will be alone.

Such consummate hegemony as we have seen in this story may continue indefinitely until an independent and capable president is elected. Usurpation of the Board can be undone if the governance committee gets restructured: does its chair offer personal initiative, and do several long term members grace the committee? If these criteria are met, then the Board's operations may return to normal. As mentioned, the Board can best return to normalcy by encouraging elections with nominations from the floor.

19. One More to Go

A SUCCESSOR

It was late May. Elections were scheduled for annual meeting the following week. Unsuccessful with the election of Frederick Jacobs in March, and Langmuir having shot down Charles Durfee at the May meeting, Talent had to scramble to find a candidate.

Phillip Penrose had joined the Board with Greta Johnson and had served an undistinguished year on Papalian's buildings and grounds committee. Talent had talked with him from time to time and determined he was presentable and sufficiently capable to be seen as an improvement over Perwick, and would be no threat to Talent's purposes.

Talent arranged for Stoddart to call the GC together to complete the election slate. As usual, Talent ran the meeting.

"We want to welcome our new member, Barbara Antlower."

Antlower spoke up, "Thank you, Bob. But where is Greta Johnson? I thought she was on the committee."

"She has stepped down."

"That means I'm alone."

"Not at all. We are all here together."

Talent continued, "John, you have served the Academy as a trustee for twelve years, and as chair of the governance committee for the last two. You are to be congratulated for this service and, I understand, it will be duly recognized at the annual meeting next week."

Stoddart responded, "Thank you, Bob. It's been a wonderful privilege for me to do so. I have enjoyed it immensely, but at the same time, I'm glad to be retiring from it."

"We have the task before us," Talent continued with his agenda, "of completing the election slate. As most of you know, I will be on it for the position of chair of this committee.

"Beth and I have talked about the importance of her continuing to make a significant contribution to the Board now that her term as president is coming to an end. We have agreed that she should be a candidate for vice-president on our slate. In that position she will be able to plan and set her own agenda of activity. Is that all right with you, Beth?"

"Yes, that will be fine."

"Is there objection to placing Beth Perwick's name on the slate for vice-president?"

There was no response from the other three.

"Thank you," said Talent to fix that item in place.

He continued, "At previous meetings we had decided that Charles Durfee would be the presidential candidate. However, I am sorry to tell you, the unfortunate explosion by Creston at the May meeting has undone that possibility. We don't want a candidate elected into a controversy over his qualifications. That would be unfair to the candidate, and might interfere with the operation of the Board.

"Last week I had a long talk with Phillip Penrose who has served well on the buildings and grounds committee for a couple of years. He is willing to take the job. He is untried, I know, but he is willing to work hard at it. He asked if I would be available to support him if need be. I informed him that I was scheduled to be the next GC chair, and that seemed to reassure him. I am convinced that he would make a good president, and I ask your concurrence in placing him on the slate for President."

Silence. No one moved or spoke.

Talent continued, "Thank you."

"If there is nothing more to be brought up, that completes our work. Meeting adjourned."

LAST LIES

The first week of June brought an air of purposeful activity about the campus as the school wound up its academic year. Langmuir escorted his son to an early awards assembly and stood about talking with his son's teachers.

The final Board meeting was later in the week.

Langmuir gave some consideration to his further interest in the Board, "Maybe this is as far as I want to go. To finish secondary school, my son is transferring out of state to a boarding school where they have a more substantial science department. I have a book in mind that I want to start writing in the

19. One More to Go

fall, and that's always a fully consuming interest. I consider the election process that will take place to be something of a charade — do I even want to watch it?"

As he walked between buildings after the ceremony, he spotted Perwick and she hailed him.

"How are you this morning, Creston?" she said. "Beautiful day isn't it?"

"I'm fine, thank you. Yes, it is a perfect June day for the activities this morning."

That was as much as Langmuir could manage. He was not willing to be so friendly as to match her personal question by responding with one of his own. But he would talk about the weather pleasantly.

Perwick put on as serious demeanor as she knew how.

"Uh oh!" thought Langmuir, "She's changing. There's that long face. I wonder what she's going to put on me now?"

"Creston," she began, "there are a couple of things I want to clarify with you."

"Yes, what are they, Beth?"

But he was thinking, "There's that wrinkled expression across her forehead that extends down the center of her face to her chin. Whatever she has in mind, it is something that's difficult for her."

"Do you remember at the Spring Fair in April, I offered to sit with you?"

"Yes I do."

"Well, I didn't mean to avoid you. It's just that Steve and I got caught up with other people, and so we never got back to you."

"I understand, Beth. Everything is forgiven. Don't worry about it."

"Thank you."

During this casual talk, Langmuir was watching her carefully.

He thought, "Is that everything? What she is saying is not true, of course. That is not what she did; that is not what happened. But why does she look like she's holding the planet on her shoulders when she's just telling a little social lie, of the kind that I generally approve of and even recommend for my own use from time to time? A little social smoothing of that sort is often to be applauded."

But Perwick was not done.

"There's another matter, Creston, I want to mention."

"Go right ahead, Beth."

He thought of adding a little levity to this morning's confessional, especially for a Catholic lady, but he thought better of it and held his tongue.

"You remember that meeting I told you about at the Harborside Inn in March?"

"Yes, of course. What about it?"

"Well, I called it."

"At last!" Langmuir thought, "This is what it's about this morning. The first episode opens the door, so to speak. This item gets driven through it."

"I don't see that it makes any difference who called it, Beth."

Langmuir was watching, "With that response, her face brightened up; no more big wrinkles. Her lips relaxed almost into the beginning of a smile."

"Well, I just wanted you to know."

"Now I know."

Perwick was done.

"I have to see some faculty now. It's been nice talking with you. See you at the meeting."

"Bye, Beth."

Perwick took off for the school's academic building.

ALONE

"So that's it," Langmuir said to himself. "Bob wants me to realize that he can go into state court and put Beth on a witness stand if need be. On the stand, under oath, she will continue her false stories, unabated, to serve his purposes, whatever those purposes may be. I don't know whether to believe that or not.

"His cohort, of course, without his even asking, will do the same, if only to confirm each other's testimony. Without my own statements on a recording machine, they could have me saying anything they wished.

"My offhand guess is that, were I to ask them, no member of the Board would be willing to testify for me. What! To submit oneself to cross questioning under oath by an antagonistic attorney, just to do Creston a favor? Not a chance.

"Even the suggestion of a possible defamation suit by Talent would bring me to an abrupt stop, were I to consider declaiming against him to the members about the means he uses to control the Board.

"Would they believe that such precise manipulation of selected individuals actually happened, or would even be possible? A few of the more experienced members, maybe. But not a majority by any means.

"There is no place for me to go. I am tired of playing the game, and have more productive activities awaiting me. With my son no longer at the school, it's time for me to leave."

19. One More to Go

BREAKING IN THE NEW MAN

Talent was determined not to repeat the mistakes he made the previous year with Perwick. He carefully debriefed Penrose to be sure he would offer no surprise nominations for the slate but, as an added precaution, he did not have Penrose meet with the GC.

The annual meeting went well. Langmuir's resignation was announced to an unresponsive Board. No attempts were made to offer candidates from the floor. The slate was adopted without a contrary word. Talent was pleased, "So, I get a third year to work undisturbed with the headmaster to update this Academy with new policy items. With Langmuir gone, the Board should be utterly quiet.

"With Beth diverted to a harmless vice-president's office, my GC has only Penrose and Antlower. The three of us should do well together.

"The several new members, as best I can tell, will take their place on the Board without feeling they have to churn things. Only one candidate had to be turned down. She was an activist in the parents association and would have been a nuisance on the Board. Fortunately, she had angered Petrillo on one occasion, so that served as a suitable argument for the GC to dismiss her."

Talent met Penrose for lunch the following week. After they were settled and had ordered, he opened the discussion, "Tell me Phil, what plans have you for the coming year?"

"Well," began Penrose, "I was just beginning to think about that. So far, I don't have any."

"Usually," said Talent, "the Board is inactive until a reception in late September. We let the school get started with its new academic year first. The headmaster, Tony Petrillo, usually begins things by having a reception to which the Board members are invited. Then the Board gets underway. The following week we have our October meeting, the first of the season."

"That sounds perfectly okay by me," responded Penrose.

"Have you looked over the Board organization sheet, to familiarize yourself with the committees, yet?" asked Talent as he dug down deep to see if there were hidden thoughts or attitudes that needed early attention.

"Yes, I have."

"Do you have concerns about it, at this point, Phil?"

"No. Not so far. But I do have one question."

"What's that?"

"How do you decide which person should be the committee chair?"

Closing Note

Why so little? Why so little reaction in these Notes to the gross behavior depicted in our story? Isn't there a more direct way to thwart a takeover attempt than the few suggestions mentioned in the chapter Notes? Why not just stop the takeover?

The difficulties are several: (1) The protagonist is a dangerous opponent; (2) The local nonprofit, or not-for-profit, or township Board is usually composed of amateurs who are not experienced directors; they may not have served previously on a Board, members are not paid, and they are at a busy stage of life of which their service to the Board may be a small part; (3) Members will tend to abhor and reject personal controversy, or the use of accusatory terms like "confederacy" and "takeover"; (4) The covert maneuvers depicted in the story are utterly foreign, hidden, and initially unbelievable to the members, just as aspects of this story may be unbelievable to the reader. A member will persuade such a Board that something is wrong only by means of a carefully arranged and presented introduction to the peril, and that takes skill and time.

The protagonist assumes from the beginning that were his plans for the organization revealed, they would get compromised or refused outright by the Board. He anticipates achieving a degree of institutional change that will require him to predominate over the management for two, four, or more years. In addition, his influence over the school headmaster must be that of a supervisor, and over the Board that of an autocrat. In the story we see how the protagonist works to achieve this influence without revealing his purpose or method.

The protagonist, in summary, uses his position as president, or usurps the president's position, to impose himself upon the headmaster, exerting a domineering influence on the operation of the school. He then protects this stance by use of his confederates to attack Board members whose presence might threaten it. While members would condemn such severe and radical methods if they knew of them, the protagonist mistakenly believes he is cleverly working just a little outside the box, within which members are doing their thinking.

The Dark Side of Leadership

An attorney, if asked how to carry out a trustee removal, will answer that it is only with considerable difficulty that one can try to dismiss a member before the end of his appointed term. The reader, however, has followed in this story the dispatch of five Board members. Those get targeted who raise questions at plenum meetings, who mention privately that something needs to be changed, who spontaneously place resolutions on the floor, or otherwise show initiative, or even those who are merely standing in the way. Because the various modes of removal usually leave behind no witnesses, they work well again and again.

The first inkling that the dark side may be at work appears as poor staffing of the governance committee or a sudden resignation. The best reaction is to talk to the chair of the GC because, if it is not disabled, that is where corrective action can and should start. If the chair will not listen, consider approaching individual GC members. If the committee is unresponsive, allow that it may be disabled. If there has been a resignation, talk to that person even though they are no longer a member, to learn if the resignation was somehow propelled. When that answer comes up positive, then a takeover looms. Responses to a takeover that deserve consideration are summarized in the paragraphs that follow.

When a takeover is underway the first step is to identify the takeover participants, the confederates. Usually, the identity of the protagonist is evident, and initially it will be the president. To undertake a takeover process without using the authority and recognition that goes with that office would be especially difficult.

To sort out the members of the confederacy, obtain Board organization charts for several previous years for reference. Talk to former officers and members, especially those of the earlier GC's. Finding out who sponsored whom to join the Board is especially important, and those whom the president sponsored are even more so. Be careful exposing to others what the questioning is about, because they may be members of the confederacy not yet identified. Mostly, watch for those patterns of behavior displayed in our story and identify the members involved. The purpose here is to create a social map of the Board that reveals the confederates.

At meetings, miss nothing! Carefully watch every detail of seating arrangements, speech, and incidental behavior. Are attempts made to interfere with a member's opportunity to speak? Does an officer or member appear to be reciting memorized words? If so, try to identify the member who benefits from those words, and add that relationship to the map. Does a member express dismay or exasperation about Board operations? If so, that member may be helpful. Is there a member of the GC whose opinions are problematic for the protagonist? Talk to him to learn his attitude. Finally, during this exploration, stay in touch with the organization's senior staff.

Since the protagonist assumed office, has the Board had a sudden resignation? Contact the resignee to see if his explanation fits the patterns shown in this story. If so, is that former member willing to meet and talk? Will he permit his story to be recorded in written or in digital form? Collect from him the details and explanations: who said what with names, and dates, and reasons why. If possible, get the text signed, along with a signed permission to use the material.

The reader who identifies the membership of a confederacy will have fulfilled the purpose of this book. The reader will have achieved a reasonable understanding of the behavior of the Board, its confederacy, and its leadership.

Unfortunately, many readers will ask themselves an enticing question: What to do about it? While the following paragraphs make several suggestions, the reader is warned that to perform them effectively depends upon the individual's practiced skills, and the reader is again warned: the protagonist may well prove a particularly dangerous opponent.

Should a member plan to do something, to become an activist, he will need one or two members as helpers. However, in acquiring these helpers there must be no inadvertent evidence of the establishment of a counter-confederacy. That would amount to a harmful misunderstanding. A mutual apprehension concerning the Board's evidently strange structure and its peculiar events determines the helper relationship.

Helpers must be willing to expose their position as a helper if they are to be useful. They should always be ready to second resolutions and speak in support of them so that, in an attempt to act from the floor of the meeting, the activist member is not left standing alone. They should be willing, when asked, to accompany the member to committee meetings, not necessarily as a participant, possibly only as a witness, to prevent the confederates from dealing with a member in complete isolation from the Board. A helper can also be useful intercepting gossip and rumors about the activist member.

At meetings, when the activist member chooses to speak, the helper must be ready to intercept harassment. When, for example, he is speaking to some matter and the confederacy makes noises, or interrupts, your helper can speak up to insist that the president enforce order on the proceedings while the speaker waits quietly for order to be established. In this way, he avoids getting pulled into a nasty word fight with the bullies, a fight that then overshadows and muffles his message.

Have an attorney available who can advise about nonprofit and township types of governance, voting procedures, and defamation avoidance. At meetings dialog might be voice recorded, in consultation with the attorney. Today, recording the plenum sessions is so easy and inexpensive that it must be considered as a retardant against planned verbal assaults. Remember, the protagonist will have friends ready to confirm having heard the activist say specific things, but that activist will have no friends to confirm his own recollections.

A first consideration if one wishes to inform the Board that a takeover is underway, concerns the activist's skills and those available among the helpers. (1) Not all of us can stand up and lead the Board rhetorically through the history of the takeover activity. (2) If you can write accurately and without defaming people, then write it out, have it professionally reviewed, and distribute it so as to lead a discussion at the next meeting. (3) Another procedure would be to introduce a resolution to the Board dealing with the difficulty, but the subject matter may be so surprising, distasteful, and foreign to many members that the vote would fail. (4) There is the recitation of short homilies about ethical behavior to, step-by-step, disarm the protagonist. (5) Finally, meet with other members individually to explain things one on one. It must be expected that each of these methods will stir the protagonist to target such an outspoken member in the various manners shown in the story.

Be prepared for surprise elections by having in mind a plausible candidate for each of the two Board offices. Brief your helpers, so they will be ready with supporting testimony. When, during seven seconds, the floor is open for nominations, gracefully enter a credible name along with a few sentences of supporting argument. That will slow the procedure, giving time for other members to contribute. If the nominated members do not object, this procedure will allow a competitive vote. Also be knowledgeable of the bylaws and insist that election rules be followed.

Should a member try to influence policy or procedures at a Board meeting, consider offering a private warning to him. The member might place a resolution on the floor calling for the minutes to be available, or might ask questions about policy items, and so forth. Recognize that such behavior makes him a target, speak to him immediately after the meeting and gently, maybe indirectly, warn him of the risk he is taking. Talk to him again a few days later to see if anything materialized. If it has, advise him not to resign, rather to bide his time.

Whenever the confederates act, they necessarily expose themselves doing so. Always try to pick up on it. Should an assault occur, take up the subject of complaint with the aggressor on the spot by asking for the history of the complaint and by asking about the possible involvement of other members in planning the assault. If questions are met with incivility, emphasize the presence of that incivility to the assembly as evidence that something has gone wrong with the Board's procedures.

If the assault takes place elsewhere, at a committee meeting or such, where you are not present, respond with alacrity when you hear of it. If the assault garnered an intent to resign, you may be in time to prevent it. Remember, the target believes the assault is a personality clash. Explain that the attack is an element of policy.

If there is a sudden resignation announcement, be sure someone responds by asking, "Why did he resign?" This should be done to get an officer's answer for the record. Visit the new resignee immediately. If the resignation was prompted, ask him to sign off on a detailed telling of the assault, the particular phrases used to hurt him, and the names of the perpetrators and witnesses. Bring the story to a meeting and do with it whatever seems possible under the circumstances. This may include identifying for the Board those who supported or initiated the assault. Initiating a Board resolution may prove a useful tactic. The resolution might provide for sending an apology to the target, or even offering reinstatement of the target. In any case, it ought to allow a complete airing of the event.

Depending — as I keep repeating — on the skills available, it may be possible to inhibit the unseemly behavior of the confederates by a few carefully spoken words at Board meetings, as in a homily. A polite complaint can be offered, for example, if meeting minutes are not available for approval, or if the agenda is without substance. Beyond such innocence, a member can offer a few sentences about unethical behavior that well behaved Boards avoid: (1) eavesdropping on a member to report what they have said privately or in a committee; (2) whispering defamations among the members, instead of leaving such matters to the professional committee; (3) interfering with speakers by engaging them in small talk or by making noise while they are speaking; (4) doing the Board's serious business outside of meetings, in the parking lot, or the next morning over the phone; and so forth. Explain that in case of requests to a member to engage in such behavior, the member must refuse and report to the professional committee with names and times of occurrence.

If the skills available are adequate to the risks provoked, more serious matters may be brought up: (1) that the governance committee is, in important ways, dysfunctional, (2) that weekly meetings of a Board member with the head of school may result in governance policy by-passing the Board; (3) that there is a confederacy working within the Board; (4) its presence requires an especially careful vetting of new member candidates; (5) how there may occur the humiliation of a member to obtain a resignation; (6) and how members should not resign if humiliated, but stay aboard to vote for a properly run Board.

What is at stake here is the old question, does the end justify the means? Where innocent Board members may assume the answer to be no, radicalized confederate members may allow the answer to be yes. Therein resides the conflict. As in our story, the Board generally never does learn of and understand the manipulating activity. The leadership contribution of other members is squashed. These tribulations will end only when, in a plenum session, the Board nominates from the floor and elects a competent president of conventional mores.

A more permanent protection from a takeover assault can be established in the bylaw details. (1) Draft them to read that the GC members are elected rather than appointed. (2) Where the bylaws give the president *ex officio* membership on every committee, the governance committee should be made an exception. The bylaws ought to provide also that upon election officers immediately take office. In this manner, for the annual meeting, the GC prepared slate might have six names: the two officers and four names for members of the GC committee. Electing the slate would result in a GC of those four members plus the chair. These changes will give a Board considerable protection against takeovers.

The protagonist, on a personal level, remains something of a wonderment. If he works for a living, from where does he get the time and energy for the numerous manipulations? Perhaps he does it as something of a hobby or pastime with a skill that makes it an offhand activity. In the example used for this book, his satisfaction comes from knowing that parents have few choices when deciding where to educate their children. Those living in the territory of our story will be educated with the student body selection, staffing, teachers, and curriculum topics for which our protagonist has arranged, whether the parents like it or not. Otherwise, the Academy will continue operating largely as before. Counter changes, if they ever happen, will take a very long time.

Finally, the reader should keep in mind that occasionally readers of this book will proclaim, "If only they knew where to find him, they would ask Robert Talent to serve with them on a current Board so as to better advance the purpose of their favorite cause."

Acknowledgments

I want to thank a number of persons who provided me with well considered critiques of the manuscript, for which effort and patience I am grateful: Frederick R. Aronson, M.D., William Glendinning, J. Howard Hannemann, M.D., Richard Hobby, Marianne Macy, Paul R. Marshall, CPA, Robert F. Preti, Esq., Carl Scovel, David C. Smith, Carolyn J. Tarr.

Author Biography

Charles Gallagher Beaudette was born and raised in the Boston area. He graduated from MIT in 1952 and then served two years in the USAF. Afterwards he did graduate studies at MIT, and practiced engineering with companies thereabout. In 1958 he founded Dychro Corporation, and after a few years of growth sold it to a computer development company.

He worked for EG&G Corp. as a senior engineer and engineering manager from 1963 to 1973, where he participated in development of one of the first digital facsimile machines with its associated telephone-line 6400 bps modem. His specialties were system design, image scanning and compression, and digital encoding for transmission. In 1973 he moved to Maine where he offered consulting services to local, national, and international firms for twelve years, retiring in 1987.

From 1989 he followed the Cold-Fusion episode which emerged that year from the University of Utah. From 1995 to 2002 he wrote two editions of *Excess Heat, Why Cold Fusion Research Prevailed*, a report on the revolutionary experimental science at the core of the subject, and the extensive theoretical controversy surrounding it. His papers from that undertaking now reside as special collection 2297 at the J. Willard Marriott Library of the University of Utah, Salt Lake City, Utah.

Mr. Beaudette has three children and lives with his wife in the village of South Bristol, Maine.

www.ingramcontent.com/pod-product-compliance
Lightning Source LLC
Chambersburg PA
CBHW071425170526
45165CB00001B/401